NORTHERN CALIFORNIA'S GUIDE FOR

Fun Excitement and Romance

NORTHERN CALIFORNIA'S GUIDE FOR

Fun Excitement and Romance

Valentine Press

By Brian Thomas Borgia

Credits:
Cover design: Faron Melrose, Inc.
Copyediting: Beverly Zegarski
Author photograph: Kevin Askeland

ISBN 0-9645476-1-9

Library of Congress Catalog Card Number: 95- 90111

DISCLAIMER:
Although the author and publisher have made every effort to ensure the accuracy and completeness of information contained in this book, we assume no responsibility for errors, inaccuracies, omissions, or any inconsistency herein. The author and publisher assume no responsibility whatsoever arising from the material contained herein or of actions of readers of this book.

Note: In this first edition, we have gone to painstaking lengths to insure that the best places to go have been included. However, if you disagree with one of our selections or have one of your own, please contact us using the form provided at the end of this book. Thank you for your purchase!

For mom, a truly remarkable woman whose love, faith, and inspiration encourages all of us.

ACKNOWLEDGMENTS

This book could have remained just a pile of notes if it were not for the help of many special people. The advisory panel, made up of family and friends, made it all possible.

A special word of thanks to my parents, Heidi, Ann, Cheri and Nonna. Without their unconditional support and new ideas, this book could not have been completed. Thank you to my grandmother whose gracious gift allowed this full-time project to begin.

Additionally, I would like to thank all the people we interviewed. Whether we were touring your place of business or receiving written information from your offices, you were wonderful.

Finally, a big thank you to Rich Weber for his assistance with the computer.

PREFACE

One of life's toughest questions is "Where do you want to go?" The question might be posed by the person you just asked out for the first time. Perhaps this inquiry came from your spouse before gearing up for a night on the town. Whoever asks this difficult question expects an answer other than "I don't know. Where do you want to go?"

In 1991, my advisory panel and I began working on ideas for a book that would provide answers to the troublesome question of where to go. We spoke with family and friends, college students and coworkers, and even people who had placed ads in the personals. We interviewed various chambers of commerce and visitor's bureaus and scoured the local entertainment weeklies for ideas.

After collecting the main ideas for the book, we began an exhaustive search to discover which businesses and what particular places should be listed under each section. Besides interviewing the people mentioned above, we went out and hiked the hiking trails, biked the bicycle paths, dined at the restaurants, and toured the hotels. At the end of our research, we had visited over 300 locations and sent out hundreds of questionnaires to local businesses.

For every activity, we have tried to include options for everyone, whether you live in San Francisco, Carmel, or anywhere in between. Businesses were included based on location and their ability to provide good service. None of the businesses listed within this book paid a fee to be included.

This book is for everyone who goes out on a date, including married couples and even two friends who may be thinking about dating. Keep your relationship exciting and life adventurous by doing something fun and romantic today.

TABLE OF CONTENTS

APPENDIXES

INTRODUCTION

The next time you ask someone out on a date or are looking for a good place to spend time with your significant other, scan through the pages of this book. Whether you are looking for a very romantic spot or just a place to have a fun and exciting time, we have detailed the perfect places to go.

Each activity is rated with romance, excitement, and cost in mind. These ratings should help guide you to the right places and activities for your specific date. For example, for a first date you may want to go someplace that is really fun and not terribly expensive. Flipping through the pages, you might find a section like "Comedy Clubs" very helpful. If you want to take your spouse of many years on a birthday date, you may find "Romantic Getaways" to be appropriate.

When you find a place you really like, make sure to write it down in the "Personal Choices" section. This will help remind you of places to which to return.

Take this book with you whenever you are traveling around the area with that special someone. Be spontaneous, adventurous, and romantic. Most of all, treasure these special times together.

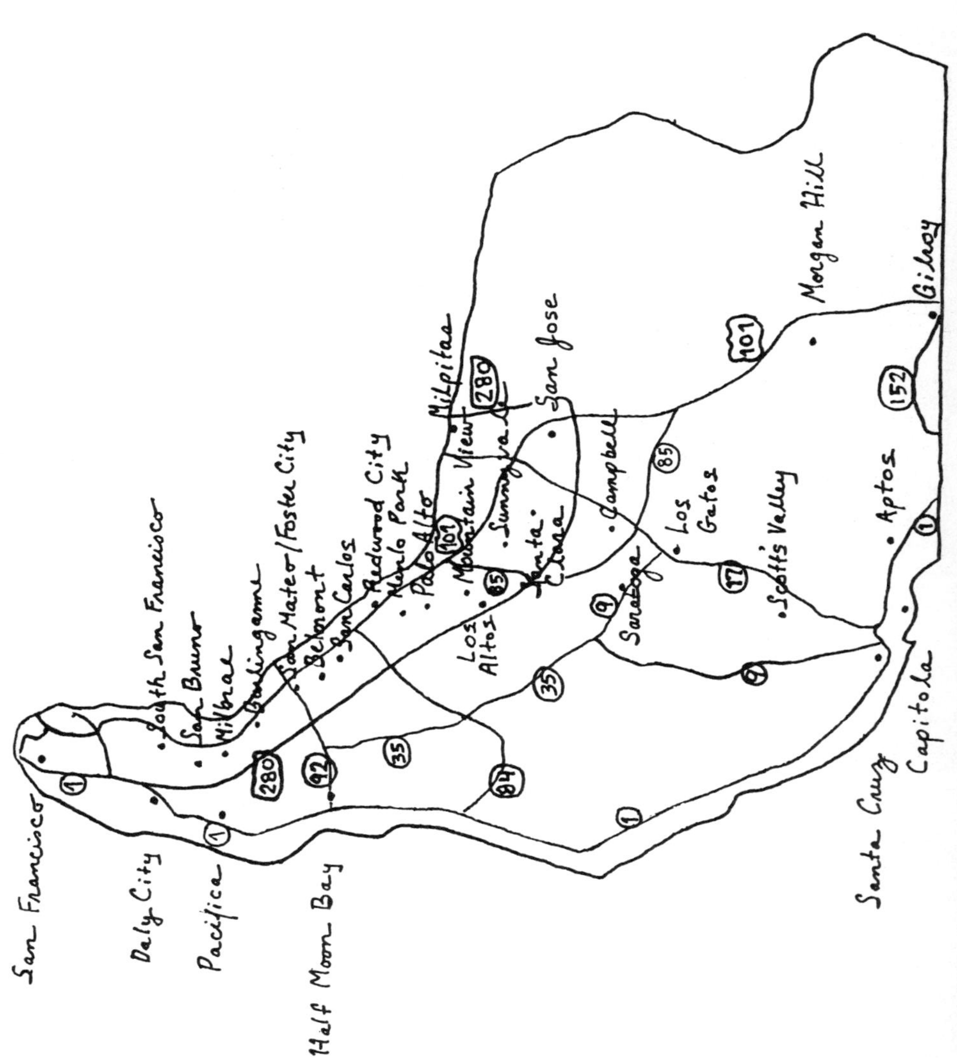
San Francisco
Daly City
Pacifica
Half Moon Bay
South San Francisco
San Bruno
Millbrae
Burlingame
San Mateo/Foster City
Belmont
San Carlos
Redwood City
Menlo Park
Palo Alto
Los Altos
Mountain View
Sunnyvale
Milpitas
Santa Clara
San Jose
Campbell
Saratoga
Los Gatos
Scotts Valley
Aptos
Santa Cruz
Capitola
Morgan Hill
Gilroy
1
280
92
35
84
101
85
9
17
152

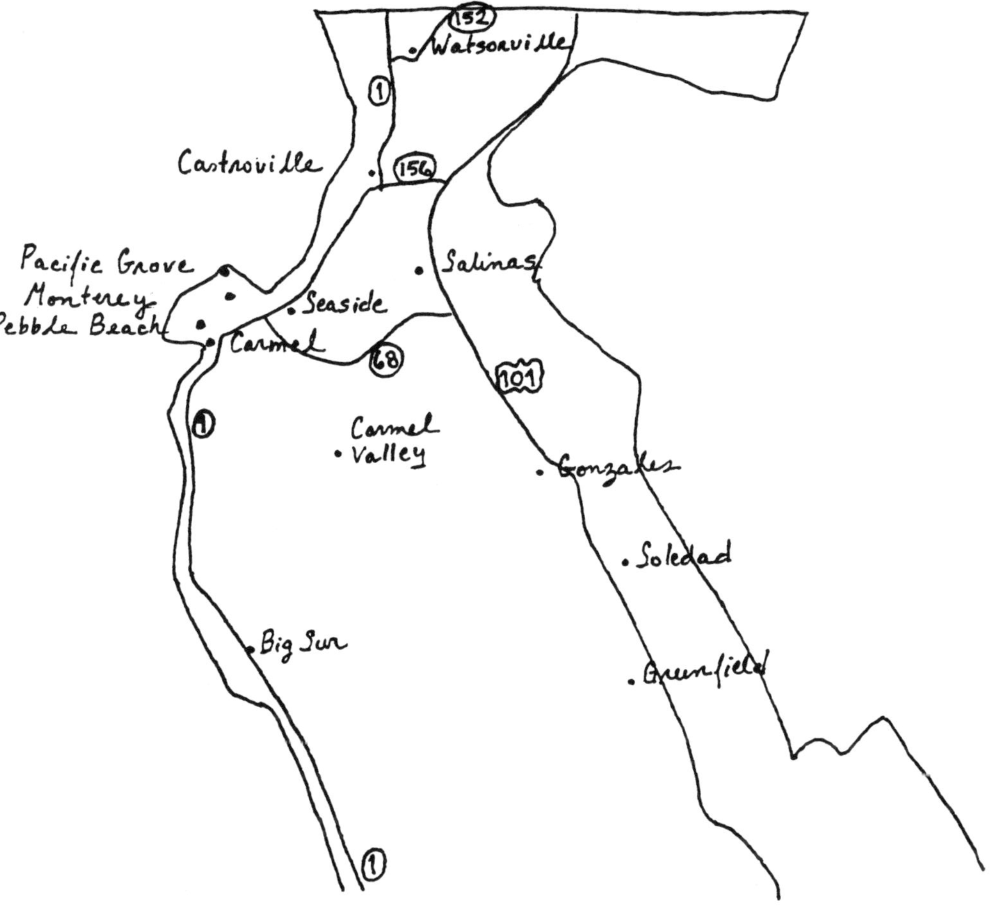
152
Watsonville
1
Castroville
156
Pacific Grove
Monterey
Pebble Beach
Seaside
Salinas
Carmel
68
101
1
Carmel
Valley
Gonzales
Soledad
Big Sur
Greenfield
1

MILEAGE CHART

(approximate miles to/from)

	San Francisco	San Jose	Santa Cruz	Monterey
San Francisco	--	45	75	120
San Jose	45	--	30	75
Santa Cruz	75	30	--	45
Monterey	120	75	45	--
Palo Alto	35	20	50	95
San Mateo	20	30	60	105
Half Moon Bay	20	40	45	90

EXPLANATION OF RATINGS

Romance Ratings

Some dating activities are more romantic than others. If you are looking for an evening of unbridled romance, taking that special someone miniature golfing or to a coffeehouse is not what you should do. The number of hearts by each section heading indicates how romantic the activities in that section are as indicated here:

♡	Friendly
♡ ♡	Somewhat romantic
♡ ♡ ♡	Romantic
♡ ♡ ♡ ♡	A romantic memory to be treasured

For example, the sections with the most romantic activities in this book are "Romantic Getaways," "Dining In," "Hot Air Ballooning," and "Weekend Getaways."

Excitement Ratings

Each activity is also rated with exclamation points to help guide you to the most exciting dating opportunities. For a date with a bit of pizzaz, check the section headings as indicated:

!	A good time
!!	More exciting than usual
!!!	Very exciting
!!!!	Knock your socks off

The most exciting section in this book is "Thrilling Activities" and includes information on hang gliding, parasailing, bungee jumping, and skydiving. Talk about your unforgettable dates!

Cost Ratings

Where you go sometimes depends on how much money you have. We have included a variety of activities that will cost you anywhere from nothing to a few hundred dollars. Remember that you do not have to spend a lot of money to have a good time.

Cost ratings are based on the average price of each activity and are not specific to each business listed in that particular section. The number of dollar signs by each section heading indicate the average cost per couple as indicated here:

$	Under $20
$$	$20 to $49
$$$	$50 to $99
$$$$	Over $100

*"Asking someone out is the easy part.
It's knowing where to go that is difficult"*

Anonymous

BEST FIRST DATES

✓Amusement places
✓Coffeehouses
✓Comedy clubs
✓Dancing
✓Fairs & Festivals
✓Ice & Roller skating
✓Miniature golf
✓Movies
✓Picnic
✓Whale Watching
✓Wine Tasting

AMUSEMENT PLACES

♡ !!! $$

Like a fountain of youth, a trip to an amusement park can make you feel like a kid again. The thrilling, grab-onto-your-seat rides, carnival games, cotton candy, and popcorn create a fun and carefree atmosphere. You can spend an entire day exploring the attractions of the park together.

Fortunately, a real diversity of amusement places are in and around the Bay Area. Thrilling roller coasters, slippery water slides and shows, nimble sprint race cars, and a mysterious house can be found nearby. From scary to tame and always entertaining, there is something for everyone.

An amusement place is a great place to go on a date. There are so many different things to do and see together. You will have many memories to share after just one afternoon.

Try to get to these amusement places early to avoid standing in long lines. Most importantly, remember to let go, relax, and have fun! Who says you can only be young once?

Amusement Places

• ***Malibu Grand Prix***, 320 Blomquist, Redwood City, (415) 367-1906. This entertainment complex offers a wide variety of recreational opportunities including three miniature golf courses, eight batting cages, two huge arcade rooms, and two sprint race car tracks. Open all year from 10 a.m.–midnight Monday–Friday and from 9 a.m.–midnight Saturday–Sunday. Each activity is priced differently and there is no charge to enter the complex.

• ***Marine World Africa U.S.A.***, Marine World Pkwy., Vallejo, (707) 643-ORCA. Killer whales, dolphins, sharks, exotic birds, Bengal tigers, and elephants are just a few of the hundreds of different animals you will see when you visit Marine World. You will also enjoy a variety of shows, an aquarium, an animal nursery, and an arcade center. Open every day during summer from Memorial Day to Labor Day and the rest of the year Wednesday–Sunday. Closed on Columbus Day, Thanksgiving, and Christmas Day. Hours: 9:30 a.m.–5 p.m. (winter), 9:30 a.m.–6 p.m. (summer), and 9:30 a.m.–5:30 p.m. (spring and fall). Please call for exact operating dates and times. Admission price of $23.95 per adult.

• ***Paramount's Great America***, Great America Pkwy. and Mission College Blvd., Santa Clara, (408) 988-1776. An amusement park that offers it all, including a stand-up roller coaster, water rides, arcade games, Broadway-style shows and concerts, and the largest 3D movie screen in the world. Open weekends during spring and fall and daily June–August. Please call for exact operating days and times. Admission price of $25.95 per adult.

• ***Raging Waters***, 2333 S. White Rd., San Jose, (408) 238-9111. Raging Waters is Northern California's premiere water theme park, featuring water slides, river rides, activity pools, and daily entertainment. A 500,000-gallon wave pool for body surfing and swimming will be added in 1995. Open mid-May–September. Please call in advance for exact dates and hours of operation. Admission price of $18.95 per adult.

• ***Santa Cruz Beach & Boardwalk***, 400 Beach St., Santa Cruz, (408) 423-5590. The only major operating beachside amusement park on the Pacific Coast, the Boardwalk features more than 50 attractions, games, and rides, including the 1924 Giant Dipper roller coaster. The park's location along the Santa Cruz Beach and near downtown Santa Cruz make it the perfect place to enjoy an entire day and evening. Open daily Memorial Day through Labor Day and weekends from September–May (closed in December). Please call for exact operating schedule. Admission is free (you pay per ride).

• ***Winchester Mystery House***, 525 S. Winchester Blvd., San Jose, (408) 247-2000. Built by rifle fortune heiress Sarah Winchester, this bizarre 160-room Victorian mansion contains several oddities such as doors to walls and stairs that lead to nowhere. Special flashlight tours on Halloween and Friday the 13th. Admission price includes a 65-minute tour of the mansion, a self-guided tour of the gardens, and two museums. Open daily (closed Christmas Day). Please call ahead for exact hours. Admission price of $12.50 per adult.

BEACHES

♡♡♡ !! $

Think for a moment about the beach. The sounds of the waves crashing onto the shore. The sight of the ocean with its many hues of blue. The feel of warm sand as your bare feet touch it for the first time. The beach can be among the most romantic places to visit depending on when you go, and what you do on this sandy paradise.

We are so lucky to live in an area where there are so many beautiful beaches. Each has its own unique character. Whether you are going out during the day for a little beach play or at sunset to snuggle by a bonfire, there is a stretch of coastline just right for you.

Beach Activities

☞ An all-day picnic & barbecue. Pack your cooler with plenty of good food and drink and head to the beach. Before you barbecue, play some beach games like smash ball or bring a football and a frisbee. Lie in the sun, take a quick dip in the ocean, and have fun. *Note: Alcohol is permitted on most beaches as long as you are over 21 and not using a glass container.*

☞ A sunset stroll. After a nice dinner in a coastal town like Santa Cruz, Monterey, or Half Moon Bay, enjoy a romantic walk along the ocean at sunset.

☞ A sunset bonfire. Bring a few pieces of wood, good kindling, and a thermos of coffee or cider to keep you warm. Snuggle under a big blanket and listen to the sounds of the ocean and a crackling fire.

☞ A run along the beach. If you have the opportunity to get a little exercise, run along the beautiful coast. It does wonders to clear the mind and relieve you of stress. Take time to stop and carve your initials in the sand.

Fifteen of the Best Beaches

Key:
[T]=Walking trails
[F]=Fires permitted in designated areas
[P]=Picnic area

Monterey County

• ***Andrew Molera State Park***. Located 20 miles south of Carmel on Hwy. 1 along the Big Sur Coast. (408) 667-2315. Several scenic trails in this 4,800-acre park lead you down to a small, secluded beach popular with surfers and equestrians. Open 9 a.m.–sunset. $4 fee. [T]

• ***Carmel Beach***. Follow Ocean Ave. off Hwy. 1 until it dead ends. Probably the most popular beach in the area, with outstanding views of Pebble Beach, a nice walking trail along the cliffs, and lots of deep, white sand. Located within a few minutes' walk of the galleries, shops, and romantic restaurants of Carmel. No fee. [T]

• ***Marina State Beach***. Exit off Hwy. 1 at Marina just north of Monterey. (408) 384-7695. Enjoy watching hang gliders leap off the sand dunes and soar like birds over the Monterey Bay. Located just 10 minutes north of downtown Monterey shops, attractions, and restaurants. Open 8 a.m. to just after sunset. No fee. [T]

• ***Monterey State Beach***. Take Del Ray Oaks off Hwy. 1. (408) 384-7695. Spectacular views of the entire Monterey Bay can be found from this enormous beach, which stretches from the municipal pier in Monterey to the town of Seaside. Open 9 a.m.–sunset. No fee. [T]

• ***Pfeiffer Beach.*** Turn right onto Sycamore Canyon Rd. (no street sign) one mile south of Pfeiffer Big Sur State Park on Hwy. 1. A mile-long road winds down through the trees to this beautiful, secluded beach surrounded by the mountains and cavernous rocks. Besides gorgeous white sands, there are opportunities for tidepooling and rock climbing. Open 6 a.m.–9 p.m. No fee. [T]

Santa Cruz County

• ***Manresa State Beach.*** Exit Hwy. 1 at San Andreas Rd. just south of Aptos. (408) 724-1266. Nearly 100 stairs lead you down to this beautiful, cliff-enclosed beach where clamming is a popular activity. Located in a residential area minutes from Capitola and Aptos. Open 8 a.m.–sunset. $6 day use fee. [T] [F]

• ***Santa Cruz Beach & Boardwalk.*** From Hwy. 1 in Santa Cruz exit at Ocean St. and follow the signs. Adjacent to California's last seaside amusement park and the municipal wharf, this beach is popular with sunbathers and volleyball enthusiasts. No fee.

• ***Seacliff State Beach***. Exit Hwy. 1 at Seacliff near Aptos. (408) 688-3222. Ride your bike, walk, or skate along the recreation trail, have a picnic and barbecue, or relax on the beach. Take a look at the old Palo Alto freighter—it is forever docked at the wharf. Open 8 a.m.–10 p.m. $6 day use fee. [T] [P]

• ***Twin Lakes State Beach***. From Hwy. 1 in Santa Cruz, take Soquel Ave. west to 7th Ave. to the coast. Watch the fishermen on the pier, the boats coming into the yacht harbor, and the ducks on Schwan Lake from this scenic beach. Near the terrific Crow's Nest restaurant (at the harbor) and downtown Santa Cruz. Open 6 a.m.–10 p.m. No fee. [F]

San Mateo County

• ***Half Moon Bay State Beach.*** All four beaches—Venice, Dunes, Roosevelt, and Francis—are located just off Hwy. 1. (415) 726-6238. The Coastside trail connects all four beaches and provides for a scenic 2.25-mile walk. Francis Beach features a large picnic area overlooking the ocean. Near downtown Half Moon Bay. Open 8 a.m.–sunset. $4 day use fee. [T] [P]

• ***Pacifica State Beach.*** Located off Hwy. 1. (415) 875-7380. For day use only, this wide, crescent-shaped beach is a quiet place to spend time after leaving San Francisco. Near the southern boundary of San Francisco. No fee.

• ***Pescadero State Beach***. Located off Hwy. 1 between Santa Cruz and Half Moon Bay. (415) 726-6238. Three different parking locations bring you to this beach, which features spectacular views from a large picnic area and from high atop the cliffs. With plenty of coves and cliffs above, it is somewhat secluded. Open 8 a.m.–sunset. No fee. [P]

• ***Waddell Beach***. Located off Hwy. 1 between Santa Cruz and Half Moon Bay. Right across the street from beautiful Big Basin Redwood State Park, this beach is a good spot to watch wind surfers tackle the ocean currents. Open 6 a.m.–sunset. No fee.

San Francisco County

• ***Baker Beach.*** Located off 25th Ave. Views of the Golden Gate Bridge and Marin Headlands surpass those of the nude sunbathers tucked away on the northern edge. No fee.

• ***China Beach***. Located off Seacliff Ave. Hike down a steep path to the foot of this tiny beach, surrounded by some of the fanciest mansions in San Francisco, and enjoy beautiful views of the Golden Gate Bridge. Located near Lincoln Park and just off scenic 49-mile drive. No fee. [T]

Bicycle Adventures

♡ !!! $

If you want to enjoy some breathtaking views from a fresh perspective, take your date on a bicycle ride. We are talking about not a ride up and down the block but an adventure on two wheels.

Travel outside your neighborhood and explore a new area. Strap your bikes onto the car or rent them at one of the bicycle shops mentioned below. Ride along the beach, through the woods, along a creek, and past small towns. Take time to drop in on a local festival, meet some new people, and enjoy the scenery.

We have tried to list trails that are fairly easy for almost anyone to ride. The more difficult trails are denoted with a "▲." For all the trails, we strongly recommend a mountain bike, a helmet, and a strong sense of adventure.

Ten Scenic Bike Trails

• ***Coyote Creek Bike Path,*** *San Jose.*
Directions: Off Hwy. 101, exit at Hellyer Ave. and go into the Hellyer Coyote County Park. Follow the main road until you reach the velodrome.
Ride distance: 14 miles Surface: Paved and dirt
Scenery: Wind along tree-lined Coyote Creek, past a large, grassy picnic area and Coyote Percolation Basin.

Start: You will notice a two-lane paved trail on your left as you head toward the velodrome. The ride starts just before the velodrome near the restrooms.
Nearby: The bike path is located within Hellyer Coyote County Park, where you can picnic by the lake, feed the ducks, and take a walk down by the creek.
Contact: (408) 225-0225 for more information.

• ***Foster City Bikeway,*** *Foster City.*
Directions: From Hwy. 101, exit at Hillsdale Blvd. Follow Hillsdale Blvd. east to Edgewater Blvd. Go left on Edgewater Blvd. and then right onto Fashion Island Blvd.
Ride distance: 9 miles Surface: Paved
Scenery: A peaceful yet windy ride around the Marina Lagoon winds around to the left and follows the edge of the San Francisco Bay past the Werder Fishing Pier and the foot of the San Mateo Bridge. Toward the end of your tour, stop to watch the big jets making final approach into SFO.
Start: From Fashion Island Shopping Center, follow Fashion Island Blvd. until just before the bridge. The pathway starts across the street on your left. Walk your bike off the trail when you see Mariners Island Blvd. and proceed south back to Fashion Island Blvd.
Nearby: The pathway winds around the residential community of Foster City. There are places to picnic and feed the ducks. Shopping and restaurants are available at Fashion Island.
Contact: Foster City Cyclery at (415) 349-2010 for more information.

• ***Golden Gate Park,*** *San Francisco.*
Directions: Follow Hwy. 1 north into San Francisco until you reach Lincoln Way or take the Great Hwy. to Martin Luther King Jr. Dr.
Ride distance: 12 miles Surface: Paved
Scenery: Your ride will wind along the streets that lead to such beautiful places as the Japanese Tea Garden, Strybing Arboretum,

and Conservatory of Flowers. Enjoy a great variety of trees and flowering plants, grassy picnic areas, and lakes.
Start: At either end of the park.
Nearby: Within the park is the California Academy of Sciences, deYoung Museum, Asian Art Museum, Japanese Tea Garden, Strybing Arboretum, and Conservatory of Flowers.
Contact: (415) 666-7200 for more information.

• ***Henry Cowell Redwoods State Park,*** *Santa Cruz County.* ▲
Directions: From Hwy. 17 north of Santa Cruz, take the Mount Herman Rd. exit. Follow this road until it ends. Take a right at the stoplight, cross a bridge, and head left onto Hwy. 9 until you reach the park.
Ride distance: 5 miles Surface: Paved and dirt
Scenery: There is a beautiful view of Santa Cruz and Monterey Bay from the observation deck (800 feet up).
Start: Head south on Pipeline Rd., turn left onto Powder Mill Trail, left onto Ridge Trail, and right onto Pipeline Rd. to the end.
Nearby: Within beautiful Henry Cowell Redwoods State Park, which comprise almost 4,000 acres, including magnificent redwoods, the San Lorenzo River and the observation deck.
Contact: (408) 335-4598 for more detailed information.

• ***Los Gatos Creek Trail,*** *Campbell and Los Gatos.*
Directions: Exit Hwy. 17 at Hamilton Ave. Head east until you reach Bascom Ave. Turn right onto Bascom and right again onto Campbell Ave. Turn left into Campbell Park, which is just past the Campbell Inn.
Ride distance: 11 miles Surface: Paved
Scenery: From Campbell Park, you will pass by Vasona Park and lake along a quiet trail with a view of the Santa Cruz Mountains.
Start: You can pick up the trail at Campbell Park.
Nearby: Quaint downtown Los Gatos and Campbell, Pruneyard shopping center, Vasona, Oak Meadow, and Campbell Parks. Plenty of places to picnic, feed the ducks, shop, eat, and meet new people.

Contact: Chamber of commerce at (408) 354-9300 for information.

• ***Monterey Recreation Trail,*** *Monterey and Pacific Grove.*
Directions: From Hwy. 1 south, exit at Del Monte/Pacific Grove. Follow Del Monte Ave. to Fisherman's Wharf.
Ride distance: 5 miles* Surface: Paved
Scenery: Ride along the Monterey Bay and pass by playful sea otters, sea lions, and harbor seals. Proceed through colorful Cannery Row and finish up at Lover's Point Park.
Start: Just to the left of the entrance to the pier at Fisherman's Wharf. Continue to Lover's Point and then return or continue on scenic Ocean View Blvd. for a longer ride.
Nearby: Fisherman's Wharf, Cannery Row, restaurants, and shops.
Contact: Adventures by the Sea at (408) 372-1807 for more information.
*The trail also runs away from Monterey toward Seaside but is a little less scenic than the short route.

• ***Purisima Creek,*** *Half Moon Bay.* ▲
Directions: From Hwy. 1 or Hwy. 92, turn onto Main St. in Half Moon Bay.
Ride distance: 13 miles Surface: Paved and dirt
Scenery: From quaint downtown Half Moon Bay, you will pass by cow pastures and agricultural fields before you reach the Purisima creek and redwoods. There is a rewarding scenic view of the coastline near the trail's end.
Start: Anywhere on main street near the Hwy. 1 intersection. Follow the bicycle lane on Hwy. 1, turn left on Verde Rd. and left onto Purisima Creek Rd. At the end of this road, there is a small parking lot on your right. You can either turn right and explore the creek, or continue to the left on Higgins Purisima Rd. back toward downtown.
Nearby: Downtown Half Moon Bay, with restaurants, coffeehouses, and shops. Several beaches are located off Hwy. 1.

Contact: The Bicyclery at (415) 726-6000 for more information.

• ***Santa Cruz to Capitola,*** *Santa Cruz and Capitola.*
Directions: From Hwy. 1 north of Santa Cruz, turn left onto Swift St., right onto Delaware Ave., and left on Swanton Blvd. toward the ocean.
Ride distance: 23 miles Surface: Paved
Scenery: Wind along the ocean front, past the Santa Cruz Beach & Boardwalk, Santa Cruz Yacht Harbor, and the town of Capitola.
Start: On West Cliff Dr. and follow it around the ocean as closely as possible to East Cliff Dr. Finish at Capitola and return the way you came.
Nearby: Santa Cruz, Capitola, and Natural Bridges State Beach.
Contact: The Bicycle Rental & Tour Center at (408) 458-3573 for more information, as there are several turns you could miss on this route.

• ***Sawyer Camp Trail,*** *San Mateo.*
Directions: From Hwy. 280, proceed west on Hwy. 92 toward Half Moon Bay and then quickly turn right onto Skyline Blvd. (Hwy. 35). Turn right onto Crystal Springs Rd.
Ride distance: 12 miles Surface: Paved
Scenery: Ride along the Crystal Springs Reservoir, past California's largest laurel tree and across the San Andreas Dam.
Start: At the entrance to the Sawyer Camp Trail.
Nearby: There are great picnic spots along the trail.
Contact: Chamber of commerce at (415) 341-5679 for more information.

• ***Stevens Canyon Road,*** *Santa Clara County.* ▲
Directions: From Hwy. 280, exit at Saratoga/Sunnyvale Rd. and head south until you reach Stevens Creek Blvd. Turn right onto Stevens Creek and left onto Foothill Blvd. This road will become Stevens Canyon Rd.
Ride distance: 12 miles Surface: Paved

Scenery: A narrow roadside bike lane twists along the trees and grassy knolls of Stevens Creek Park and Reservoir.
Start: Along Stevens Canyon Rd. near the first entrance to Stevens Creek Park. Follow Stevens Canyon Rd. off to the right and then return the way you came after the road dead ends.
Nearby: Downtown Saratoga, Hakone Japanese Gardens, wineries.
Contact: Stan's Bicycle Store at (408) 996-1234 for more information.

Bicycle Shops Located Near the Above Trails

• ***Action Sports***, 1777 Hillsdale Blvd., San Jose, (408) 978-8383. Rentals: $5–$8 per hour or $15–$30 per day. Tandem bikes available.

• ***Adventures by the Sea***, 299 Cannery Row, Monterey, (408) 372-1807. Rentals: $6 per hour or $24 per day. Tandem bikes available.

• ***The Bicycle Rental & Tour Center,*** 415 Pacific Ave., Santa Cruz, (408) 426-8687. Rentals: $4–$8 per hour or $25–$50 per day. Tandem bikes available.

• ***The Bicyclery***, 432 Main St., Half Moon Bay, (415) 726-6000. Rentals: $6 per hour. or $24 per day.

• ***Foster City Cyclery***, 999-B Edgewater Blvd., Foster City, (415) 349-2010. Rentals: $8 per hour or $30 per day.

• ***Golden Gate Park Bike & Skate***, 3038 Fulton St., San Francisco, (415) 668-1117. Rentals: $5 per hour or $25 per day. Tandem bikes available.

• ***Mikes Bikes & Blades***, Golden Gate Park Stow Lake, San Francisco, (415) 668-6699. Rentals: $5–$7 per hour or $18–25 per day.

• ***Stan's Bicycle Store***, 19685 Stevens Creek Blvd., Cupertino, (408) 996-1234. Rentals: $20 per day.

CARRIAGE RIDES

♡♡♡ !! $

We have chapters on scenic drives, hikes, and bicycle rides, but no form of transportation is more romantic than a horse-drawn carriage. Without the roar of a 130-horsepower engine, your two horsepower carriage leads you with only the "click-clack" sound of horseshoes meeting the pavement.

A carriage ride is truly a magical experience. As you ride through town, people will wave and smile at you, and the stars will seem to sparkle just a bit brighter than usual. The carriage will inch forward slowly as you cuddle with your date under a warm blanket.

As you near the end of your journey, have your picture taken so that you will forever remember this night. Afterwards, enjoy a warm cup of coffee at a local cafe or a drink at a nearby bar.

Carriage Rides

• ***Los Gatos***, downtown Los Gatos, (408) 354-9300. Enjoy a horse-drawn ride along the quaint main streets of Los Gatos in a variety of carriages. Available only during December on the first three weekends. Cost: $10 per person.

• ***Santa Cruz***, downtown Santa Cruz, (408) 425-1234. Take a trip through downtown Santa Cruz the old-fashioned way. Available only during late November–December (Thursday-Sunday) but a summer schedule is in the works. Cost: $5 per person.

• ***San Francisco***, Pier 33 on the Embarcadero, (415) 398-0857. Travel along the waterfront in a romantic, 19th-century-style horse-drawn carriage. Rides through other areas of the city are available by arrangement. Call for current cost and availability.

COFFEEHOUSES

♡ ! $

Going out for coffee has changed a lot over the past several years. Simple cafes have been replaced by coffeehouses that feature a variety of specialty coffee drinks, live entertainment, and a generous assortment of desserts. To ask someone out for coffee can be special.

From the moment you walk through the coffeehouse door, you will experience the pleasant aroma of freshly ground coffee. After ordering a specialty coffee like a cafe latte, double mocha, or cafe Borgia, find a table for two and relax. Talk about politics, world affairs, sports, or your relationship and get to know each other a little better. Some people like to just sit back and "people watch."

Going out for coffee is a great first date because it gives you the best chance to get to know someone new. Compared to bars, these places are quieter, and caffeine does not impair your judgment like a rum and coke might. All in all, coffeehouses provide the best (tasting) forum for communication.

Neighborhood Coffeehouses

• ***Caffe Cardinale Roasting Company***
Ocean Avenue, Carmel, (408) 626-2095.

• ***Caffe Roma***
414 Columbus, San Francisco, (415) 391-8584.

• ***Campbell Coffee Roasting Company***
1875 S. Bascom Ave. at the Pruneyard, Campbell, (408) 559-8040.

• ***The Coffee Club***
1035 Ralston Ave., Belmont, (415) 591-9888.

• ***The Coffee Critic***
1407 Burlingame Ave., Burlingame, (415) 343-4434.

• ***The Coffee Critic***
106 S. El Camino Real, San Mateo, (415) 342-8558.

• ***Coffee Roasting Company***
17400 Monterey Rd., Morgan Hill, (408) 778-2586.

• ***Coffee Society***
21269 Stevens Creek Blvd., Sunnyvale, (408) 725-8091.

• ***Fred's Coffee Roasting***
29 N. San Pedro, San Jose, (408) 298-8040.

• ***International Coffee Exchange***
14471 Big Basin Way, Saratoga, (408) 741-1185.

• ***LA DI DA***
Purissima and Kelly Sts., Half Moon Bay, (415) 726-1663.

• ***Los Gatos Coffee Roasting Company***
101 W. Main St., Los Gatos, (408) 354-3263.

• ***Main Street Coffee Roasting Company***
1112 Main St., Redwood City, (415) 368-3430.

• ***Mr. Toots***
221-A Esplanade, Capitola, (408) 475-3679.

• ***Nepenthe***
Hwy. 1 30 miles south of Carmel, Big Sur, (408) 667-2345.

• ***Pacifica Java Cafe***
450 Dondee Way, Pacifica, (415) 738-1222.

• ***Pacific Grove Coffee Roasting***
510 Lighthouse Ave., Pacific Grove, (408) 655-5633.

• ***Palo Alto Coffee Roasting Company***
At Stanford Shopping Center, Palo Alto, (415) 327-2233.

• ***Peet's Coffee & Tea***
899 Santa Cruz Ave., Menlo Park, (415) 325-8989.

• ***Red Rock Coffee Company***
201 Castro St., Mountain View, (415) 967-4473.

• ***Samsara***
400 Alvarado St., Monterey, (408) 373-5282.

• ***Santa Cruz Coffee Roasting Company***
1330 Pacific, Santa Cruz, (408) 459-0100.

• ***Spanky's***
632 San Mateo Ave., San Bruno, (415) 588-8438.

• ***Starbucks***
296 Main St., Los Altos, (415) 949-3565.

• ***Starbucks***
1899 Union, San Francisco, (415) 921-4049.

• ***Starbucks***
El Camino Real, Santa Clara, (408) 984-7174.

"Among those whom I like or admire, I can find no common denominator, but among those whom I love, I can: all of them make me laugh"

W.H. Auden

Comedy clubs

♡ !!! $

Has life been treating you rough lately? Nothing to smile about? Maybe it's time you spent a few hours laughing in one of the area's spectacular comedy clubs.

We all need to laugh, whether it be about work, ourselves, or our family. Comedy shows provide that opportunity with styles of humor to please most everyone. From racy to clean, nationally recognized comedians are ready to help you take life a little less seriously.

Going to a comedy club is a great first date because of the relaxing, feel-good environment where people have left their worries behind. A little laughter also helps to "break the ice" and takes some of the pressure off you. After the show, you can go out for coffee or drinks, remember a few jokes, and get to know each other a little better.

Comedy Clubs

• ***Cobb's Comedy Club***, 2801 Leavenworth St., San Francisco, (415) 928-4320. Comfortable 185-seat club located adjacent to an Italian restaurant, which provides guests good food in the comedy room. Quality shows with no "cheap shots." Shows at 8 p.m. Monday, 9 p.m. Tuesday–Sunday and a second show on the weekends at 11 p.m. $8–$15 plus a two-beverage minimum.

• ***ComedySportz***, 3428 El Camino, Santa Clara, (408) 985-LAFF. A competitive team comedy that is completely improvised based on audience suggestions. Two teams engage in a battle of wits, with the audience determining the winner. No drink minimum and no offensive material. Shows Friday at 9 p.m. and Saturday at 8 p.m. and 10 p.m. $7 admission.

• ***Giggles Comedy Club & Restaurant***, 1380 Industrial Rd., San Carlos, (415) 595-3319. Spacious 350-seat club featuring a full bar and restaurant. Shows Tuesday–Thursday at 8 p.m. (8:30 p.m. July–September) and a second show Friday and Saturday at 10:30 p.m. (10:45 p.m. July–September). $6 weekdays and $10 weekends.

• ***Knuckleheads***, 150 S. First St., San Jose, (408) 998-4242. Located in the San Jose Live! entertainment complex downtown, Knuckleheads offers top performers in a lively atmosphere. Shows Sunday–Thursday at 8 p.m. and Friday and Saturday at 8 p.m. and 10 p.m. $5 weekdays and $8 weekends (includes free admission into San Jose Live!).

• ***Last Laugh***, 29 N. San Pedro St., San Jose, (408) 287-LAFF. Enjoy the performances of three to four comedians each night in this comfortable club in downtown San Jose. Shows Wednesday, Thursday and Sunday at 8 p.m. and Friday and Saturday at 8 p.m. and 10:30 p.m. Cover varies and there is a two-drink minimum.

• ***The Punch Line***, 444 Battery St., San Francisco, (415) 397-7573. Probably the most popular and most cosmopolitan comedy club in our area. The Punch Line features some of the best comedians in the country. Because of its extreme popularity, purchasing show tickets in advance is advised. Call for times/fees.

• ***Rooster T. Feathers***, 157 W. El Camino, Sunnyvale, (408) 736-0921. A cross between an 1890s saloon and 1930s art deco, this 3,000 square foot club features top name performers and the largest cocktail selection of any comedy club. Shows Tuesday–Sunday at 8:30 p.m. and a second show Friday and Saturday at 10:30 p.m. $7 weekdays and $10 weekends.

CONCERTS

♡♡ !!! $$$

Some people say that listening to a compact disc on your stereo system is just like being at a live concert. Who are they kidding? Although technology has advanced, there is no substitute for seeing your favorite band perform in person.

Depending on who you see perform, your experience will be different. Guns and Roses or Aerosmith will give a wild show, and the crowd will go crazy. A Whitney Houston or Kenny G concert might be a little subdued and better suited for a romantic mood. At every special event like this, hundreds or thousands of people will join you in welcoming some of the finest music entertainers.

Get to the show early so you do not miss one guitar chord, one bar of notes, or one high-pitched scream from the lead singer. Together, you and your date can enjoy sharing your great taste in music.

Note: Concert tickets can be conveniently purchased through BASS. They can also be contacted for current event information at (408) 998-BASS and (510) 762-BASS.

Places to See a Major Concert Event

• ***The Catalyst***, 1011 Pacific Ave., Santa Cruz, (408) 423-1336. The vanguard of the south bay rock scene, The Catalyst brings in top performers like Michael Hedges, Midnight Oil, Gregg Allman, and Chris Isaak.

• ***Event Center***, Seventh and San Carlos Sts., San Jose, (408) 924-6333. Located on the campus of San Jose State University, the Event Center has featured Jethro Tull, Black Sabbath, and Nine Inch Nails.

• ***The Fillmore***, 1805 Geary Blvd. at Fillmore, San Francisco, (415) 346-6000. A full service restaurant and bar that also offers the best in music entertainment. Top performers in 1994 included Eric Clapton, Huey Lewis & the News, Johnny Cash, and the Spin Doctors.

• ***Great American Music Hall***, 859 O'Farrell St. at Polk, San Francisco, (415) 885-0750. More of a cabaret-style music club, the Great American Music Hall presents the best of the blues, rock, jazz, and country performers.

• ***The Mountain Winery***, 14831 Pierce Rd. at Hwy. 9, Saratoga, (408) 741-5182. A small, intimate outdoor retreat with beautiful views of the mountains, valleys, and vineyards. Last year's summer series featured performances by Taylor Dayne, Tom Jones, Wynton Marsalis, Paul Anka, and The Tubes. Various music festivals also take place there from the blues to folk.

• ***Orpheum Theater***, 1192 Market St. at Hyde, San Francisco, (415) 474-3800. The Orpheum features Broadway musicals, world class comics and the world's finest musicians, including Tony Bennett, Steve Lawrence and Eydie Gorme.

• ***Redwood Amphitheater***, Great America Pkwy off Hwy 101, (408) 988-1776. Located within Paramount's Great America, the

Redwood Amphitheater presents big name entertainment at a very reasonable cost.

• ***San Jose Arena,*** W. Santa Clara and Autumn Sts., San Jose, (408) 287-9200. Eighteen-thousand-seat home of the San Jose Sharks. Recent performances by Janet Jackson, The Eagles, Barbara Streisand, Elton John, and Eric Clapton.

• ***Shoreline Amphitheater***, N. Shoreline Blvd., Mountain View (415) 967-4040. Some of the biggest concert events of the year take place on their large outdoor stage surrounded by preferred and lawn seating. Concerts in 1994 featured such names as the Grateful Dead, Aerosmith, Michael Bolton, Wyonna, and Phil Collins.

• ***Slim's***, 333 11th St. at Folsom, San Francisco, (415) 621-3330. Boz Scagg's club features all kinds of music from performers like Sheryl Crow, Chris Isaak, and Gregg Allman.

• ***The Warfield***, 982 Market St. between 5th and 6th, San Francisco, (415) 775-7722. Built in the early 1920s, The Warfield provides a unique and comfortable concert venue with its cathedral ceiling and opulent decor. Jerry Garcia, Joe Jackson, The Pretenders, and Seal were featured in 1994.

"A woman knows the face of the man she loves as a sailor knows the open sea."

Honore de Balzac

CRUISING THE PACIFIC

 !!! $$$

If you are from this area, chances are you have been on a boat at least once. Maybe you were fishing or whale watching or sailing on the ocean. For a truly romantic rendezvous, travel first class across the big blue with one of the charter companies listed below.

Your choices vary from a three-hour dinner cruise in San Francisco to a daytime sailing expedition across the Monterey Bay or Sunday brunch on a luxury yacht. If you want to do something different, get yourselves some sea legs and enjoy a wonderful time complete with fresh air, unparalleled views, impeccable service, and marvelous cuisine.

If you choose to go on one of the dinner dance cruises, consider the option of staying over at one of the romantic hotels listed on pages 107–114. Sleep in, have breakfast in bed, and then continue to explore the land.

Charter Companies

• ***Blue & Gold Fleet***, Pier 39 on the Embarcadero, San Francisco, (415) 781-7877. They offer many cruises, including a one-and-a-quarter-hour bay cruise and a three-hour dinner dance cruise. The dinner dances take place Friday & Saturday evenings from April–December at a cost of $40 per person.

• ***Chardonnay Sailing Charters***, Santa Cruz Yacht Harbor, Santa Cruz, (408) 423-1213. The *Chardonnay II*, a sleek 70-foot racing style yacht, really moves! They offer several excursions, including sunset sails and wine tasting cruises for $36 per person including snacks. A cross-the-bay champagne brunch cruise sails to Monterey and returns you to Santa Cruz via limousine for $59 per person.

• ***Hornblower Dining Yachts***, Pier 3 on the Embarcadero, San Francisco, (415) 788-8866. The largest dining cruise company on the West Coast, Hornblower offers elegant dinner dance cruises ($34.95–$65 per person), champagne brunch cruises ($29–$36 per person), and a wild reggae cruise. Please call for availability.

• ***Pacific Marine Yachts***, Pier 39 on the Embarcadero, San Francisco, (415) 788-9100. Their fleet of four elegantly appointed yachts, featuring award winning gourmet cuisine, is a perfect option for the ultimate romantic adventure. They offer a Sunday brunch cruise for $40 per person and a dinner dance cruise for $62–$80 per person. Call for a quarterly event calendar.

• ***Pacific Yachting***, 333 Lake Ave., Santa Cruz, (408) 476-2370. They offer private charters for six or less passengers that sail past the Santa Cruz Boardwalk to the quaint town of Capitola. Enjoy a meal on board or shuttle into town for a romantic dinner. Cost for two passengers ranges from $140 for two hours to $400 for six hours on a 25-foot luxury yacht. Please call for availability.

• ***Rendezvous Charters***, Pier 40, S. Beach Harbor, San Francisco, (415) 543-7333. Leap back about 60 years and come aboard the 78-foot *Brigantine Rendezvous* tall ship. On this historic vessel, they offer a brunch cruise ($39 per person, Sundays from 11 a.m.–2 p.m.), sunset cruise ($22.50 per person, two hours prior to sunset), and dinner cruise (from $45 per person, nightly from 7:30 p.m.–10 p.m.).

• ***Spinnaker Sailing***, Port of Redwood City, 451 Seaport Ct., Redwood City, (415) 363-1390. For the ultimate in private sailing, charter a boat for the two of you or up to three couples and cruise the San Francisco Bay. Sailboats range in size from 22 to 32 feet. Please call at least one week in advance for reservations. Cost for up to six passengers ranges from $114 to $207 for a half day, including a skipper.

MOST EXCITING DATES

- ✓Amusement places
- ✓Concert
- ✓Dancing
- ✓Day at the races
- ✓Hot air ballooning
- ✓Kayaking
- ✓Pro sporting events
- ✓Thrilling activities

DANCING

♡♡ !!! $

The energy in a dance club is amazing. No matter if you are going out to rock and roll, do the two-step, or waltz to a ballroom beat, good music and fun people mix together for an exciting evening. There is something about dancing that just makes you feel good.

We have listed some of the most popular dance clubs in our region. They offer different styles of music, some of which you may not be too familiar with. If you are use to rock and roll, try learning how to line dance for a change of pace. Several clubs offer a night or two a week of dance lessons for just the cost of the cover.

Whether you are out on a first date or have been dating for years, it is always fun to take a group of friends along for the night. Take a limousine or taxi to a couple of different clubs and make it a fun night to remember.

Dance Clubs

San Francisco County

• ***Harry Denton's***, 161 Steuart St. at Harbor Court Hotel, San Francisco, (415) 882-1333. A beautiful view of the Bay is not the only reason people come to Harry Denton's. People also go there for the great restaurant, saloon, and live R&B music as well as DJ dancing every Thursday–Saturday.

• ***Johnny Love's***, 1500 Broadway at Polk, San Francisco, (415) 931-6053. One of the more popular spots in the city, Johnny Love's features a giant bar, excellent American cuisine, and dancing to live rock and blues music.

• ***Lou's Pier 47 Club***, 300 Jefferson St. at Jones, San Francisco, (415) 771-0377. A great restaurant on the wharf and great dancing upstairs to live music ranging from country rock to the blues.

• ***Oz***, Westin St. Francis Hotel, 32nd Floor, 335 Powell St. at Geary, San Francisco, (415) 774-0116. Listen to top 40 and international modern music in style from high atop the city. Appropriate dress required.

Note: If you want to hit a lot of clubs in one area of San Francisco, check out the south of market street area. There you will find ***Club DV8*** (540 Howard St. between 1st & 2nd), ***DNA Lounge*** (375 11th St. at Harrison), ***Club 1015*** (1015 Folsom St. at 6th), ***Paradise Lounge*** (1501 Folsom St. at 11th St.), and the ***Sound Factory*** (525 Harrison St. at First).

Santa Clara County

• ***Cheers***, 685 E. El Camino, Sunnyvale, (408) 749-1288. This bar and dance club does not look exactly like the Cheers bar on television, but everyone is just as friendly as Sam and Woody. Come as you are and enjoy dancing to live rock and roll and country and western. You can also learn a few steps from their dance instructor from 7-9 p.m. Monday and Tuesday.

• ***Club Oasis***, 200 N. First St., San Jose, (408) 292-2212. Located in the heart of downtown San Jose, Club Oasis features DJ dancing to house techno and live performances. In this multi-level club, there is dancing on two floors, five bars, and four pool tables.

• ***F/X The Club***, 400 South First St., San Jose, (408) 298-9796. Celebrating their fifth year, the best DJ's in the area spin music ranging from acid jazz to hip-hop and funk. There is always a party happening at F/X.

• ***J.J. Blues Downtown***, 14 S. Second St., San Jose, (408) 286-3066. The premier blues club in San Jose, J.J.'s offers dancing to live music ranging from the blues to rock and roll to reggae. It's like going to a concert with a large dance floor.

• ***The Palace***, 146 South Murphy Ave., Sunnyvale, (408) 739-5179. Formerly a movie cinema and beautifully restored into an intimate, art nuveau dance club, the Palace is beyond compare. From Wednesday-Saturday nights they feature live and DJ music ranging from salsa and swing to contemporary.

• ***The Saddle Rack***, 1310 Auzerais Ave., San Jose, (408) 286-3393. The Saddle Rack offers the best in country and western dancing. Enjoy two live bands on the weekends, three dance floors, thirteen bars and a ride on the mechanical bull.

• ***San Jose Live!***, Pavilion Shops, 150 South First St., San Jose, (408) 294-5483. Step inside their boxing ring at this sports bar and entertainment complex and grove to the sounds of top 40 music. Afterwards, enjoy the comedy club, full-service restaurant and piano bar.

San Mateo County

• ***Bobby McGee's***, Crown Sterling Suites, 250 Gateway Blvd., Burlingame, (415) 342-4600. At this popular restaurant and lounge you are sure to run into a host of storybook characters waiting on you. Their DJ's play a wide variety of music spanning the twentieth century.

• ***The Edge***, 260 California Ave., Palo Alto, (415) 324-EDGE. If you like listening to Live 105 music then you will love this club. On dance nights, they play mostly modern rock along with techno and top 40 music. This 18 and older dance club is *the* dance club to go to between San Francisco and San Jose.

Santa Cruz County

• ***The Catalyst***, 1011 Pacific Ave., Santa Cruz, (408) 423-1336. This large Mediterranean style dance club features dancing to live bands most every night ranging from rock and roll to reggae and everything in between. Every Monday-Wednesday nights there are cabaret performances in their beautiful atrium. Besides dancing, there are two bars, a restaurant, and a pool hall.

• ***Moe's Alley,*** 1535 Commercial Way, Santa Cruz, (408) 479-1854. Enjoy dancing to the sounds of live blues music from this recently renovated and expanded bar and dance club. You will definitely feel at home at this friendly, intimate club where everyone has a great time.

Monterey County

• ***Brasstree Lounge***, Doubletree Hotel, #2 Portola Plaza, Monterey, (408) 649-4511. Located on the top floor of the hotel, the Brasstree offers dancing to a variety of live music from 50's and 60's rock and roll to jazz. From their location, you will also enjoy spectacular views of the Monterey Bay.

• ***Doc Ricketts' Lab***, 95 Prescott, Monterey, (408) 649-4241. Located on historic Cannery Row, Doc Ricketts' Lab, a basement style bar and dance club, presents a mix of live blues and modern music from some of the top bands around.

• ***Nick's Place***, 180 E. Franklin St., Monterey, (408) 372-2244. Nick's is a high energy, stylish club in downtown Monterey with DJ dancing to sounds ranging from country to R&B.

DAY AT THE RACES

♡ !!! $

When we first arrived at the main gate of Bay Meadows Racecourse, we thought we had made a mistake. Why would someone want to take a date to the racetrack? Isn't it a dirty place filled with old guys who like to gamble?

We were wrong. There are some people there who are a little too excited about gambling, but the track is a really fun and exciting place to go. People are cheering, and the announcer is screaming as the horses race around the track toward the finish. After just one race, you get caught up in all of it.

If you choose to go, we highly recommend a seat in the turf club. This area is fairly private, is very clean, and offers one of the best views of the track. The additional cost of $18 is well worth it.

Take a chance and place a bet on a race or two. A program available at the front gate for 50 cents explains all you need to know. Perhaps you will both walk away richer for the experience in more ways than one.

Bay Meadows Racecourse. From Hwy. 101, proceed on Hwy. 92 toward Half Moon Bay and exit at S. Delaware. Head south until you reach the main gate. (415) 574-RACE. Live racing from August–January, every Wednesday–Sunday from 12:30–5 p.m. General admission price of $3.00.

Valentino's

I Primi

★Steamed artichoke with herbed mayonnaise
★Antipasto of fresh vegetables, sliced meats, and cheeses

La Pasta

★Angel hair pasta with tomato, garlic, fresh herbs, and parmesan cheese

I Secondi

★Veal scallopini

I Dolci

★Assortment of gelato and biscotti
★Espresso

Tonight's wine: Chianti Romanelli (1991)

DINING IN

 !! $$

Sometimes it is better not to go out. Why not stay at home and romance your partner with a specially prepared, creatively themed dinner? Believe me, it will leave more of an impression than a night at even the fanciest of restaurants.

Perhaps you are not the best cook in the world. You can tailor the meal to fit your talents and make it work. Your date will appreciate your efforts and love you for your creativity.

Ideas for Dining In

• ***Theme Dinner***. Transform your apartment or home into a restaurant. Perhaps your dining partner has a preference for Chinese or Indian food. Instead of bringing them to a restaurant, impress them at home. For example, let's put together an Italian restaurant theme complete with menu and decor. Here is what you will need:

- Music (classical Italian variety or Madonna if you can't stand vintage music).
- Red-and-white checkered tablecloth.
- Candles.
- Fresh flowers (red roses or carnations are nice).
- A good Italian meal. If you cannot cook, pick up an order from a local restaurant.
- A nice bottle of Chianti wine or sparkling cider.
- Decorations. You can decorate the front door and the

inside of your place to resemble a real Italian restaurant. The more detailed you get, the better the presentation.
• A keepsake menu (see page 44).

Remember to take a picture during dinner. This will be a romantic evening that is not soon forgotten.

• ***Formal Dinner***. The key to a good formal dinner is presentation. A nicely set table and well thought out meal go a long way. A few suggestions:

• Music (slow and romantic).
• Candlelight.
• Fresh flowers.
• The best tablecloth (white) and dishes you can find. If you cannot find two plates that match, consider heavy Chinette paper plates.
• A nice bottle of wine or sparkling soda.
• Good food. Once again, if you can't cook then order out or use a catering service. Getting frustrated before and during dinner will make you upset after dinner.
• If you do cook, try a dish that your date will enjoy. Serving meat to a vegetarian will show a lack of sensitivity (and a freezer full of leftovers).
• Do not forget dessert. Fresh strawberries and cream or a chocolate fondue are fun. A flaming dessert like flambe Raspberry or Bananas Foster is easy to make and looks and tastes great.
• Dress nicely for the occasion. Request that your date wear something semiformal. At least tell them to give the old jeans and tee shirt a break.

Afterwards, a little dancing by the fireplace or a moonlight stroll adds a nice finishing touch to the evening.

• ***Home Beach***. This idea is a little more time consuming, but well worth it. If you are in a location where the beach is far away, simply bring a piece of the beach to your home.

The goal is to create a little section of beach on your deck, patio, or back porch. A list of things that you will need:

- A few large bags of sand
- Tarp (to place sand on—easier for cleanup)
- Two beach towels
- Pine cones, leaves, shells, kelp...anything normally found on a beach
- Sounds of the ocean tape or compact disc
- Beach chairs
- Beach umbrella
- Barbecue

Again, presentation is the key to a successful evening. Lead your date out onto your mock beach with the sounds of the ocean playing in the background. Step out onto the cool sand. Serve a nice tropical drink. Barbecue dinner and toast somemores for dessert.

If the weather outside is cold, you may consider using a couple of charcoal starter cylinders as small fire rings. Fill them up with charcoal and make sure to keep them away from anything flammable. Set them on top of your barbecue or another safe place like on top of brick or cement blocks.

• ***Carpet Picnic***. One of the easiest indoor dinners to prepare is a carpet picnic. Although the idea is self explanatory, here are a few tips:

- Lay out a large, comfortable blanket in front of your fireplace or a window.
- Purchase a selection of fruits and cheeses, crackers, French bread or croissants, deli meats and a salad.

• Enjoy a nice bottle of wine or sparkling soda.
• Have some good music to listen to or a good movie to watch.

More ideas for a picnic can be found on page 95.

DINING OUT

♡♡♡ ! $$$

When you take that someone special out to one of these restaurants, you are taking them out on a dining experience they will not soon forget. All of the restaurants listed below have passed our "romantic test" with flying colors.

What gives a particular establishment a romantic feel? Fresh flowers and soft candlelight are a nice start. Add a spectacular view or marvelous location, outstanding personal service, and magnificent cuisine and you are almost there. Make it all worth the price paid, and you have found a romantic restaurant that stands above all others.

After dinner, go dancing, take a scenic drive, or have tickets in hand for the theater. Perhaps you are celebrating a special anniversary. Check out our listings for "Romantic Getaways" to find a nearby hotel or inn to continue your romantic evening together.

Although all of these restaurants offer a romantic atmosphere, there are others out there that you may visit and enjoy. Make sure to write them down in the "Personal Choices" section.

The number of dollar signs following the description of each restaurant indicates the average dinner cost, not including wine, tax, and gratuity, per couple, as indicated below:

$$: Less than $40 $$$: Between $40–$60 $$$$: Over $60

Twenty Romantic Restaurants

• ***Anton & Michel***, Mission and Seventh Sts., Carmel, (408) 624-2406. An elegant setting with classic white pillars and a window wall overlooking the "court of fountains" provide for a classic dining experience. A friendly staff serves a marvelous Continental cuisine, including salads, meats and desserts prepared tableside. Near downtown Carmel. Open for dinner nightly from 5:30–9:30 p.m. $$$

• ***Baccarat*** at Hotel Sofitel, 223 Twin Dolphin Dr., Redwood City, (415) 598-9000. A view of the lagoon, elegant decor, and soft music help set the mood for romance in this formal, fine dining restaurant serving French cuisine. Located near the San Francisco Bay. Open for dinner nightly from 6 p.m. $$$

• ***Bella Vista***, 13451 Skyline Blvd., Woodside, (415) 851-1229. Built in 1927, this restaurant has the feel of an old French country inn set among the redwoods. Stunning views of the South Bay Area, wonderful Continental cuisine, and a crackling fireplace make this a perfect place for a special occasion. Located near Half Moon Bay and Palo Alto. Open for dinner Monday–Saturday from 5 p.m. $$$

• ***Cafe Majestic***, 1500 Sutter St., San Francisco, (415) 776-6400. Located in the Majestic Hotel, Cafe Majestic offers a perfect blend of California and European cooking served in the romantic atmosphere of Old San Francisco. Open for dinner nightly from 5:30–10 p.m. $$$

• ***Campbell House Restaurant,*** 106 E. Campbell Ave., Campbell, (408) 374-5757. Located in a charming 65-year-old-house, this tiny restaurant offers New American cuisine in a comfortable homelike atmosphere. Attentive service, delicious food, and a good value make this a must place to visit. Located near old downtown Campbell. Open for dinner Tuesday–Friday from 6– 9:30 p.m., Saturday and Sunday from 5:30 p.m. $$$

• ***The Carnelian Room***, 555 California St., San Francisco, (415) 433-7500. Located in the Bank of America building, the Carnelian Room offers breathtaking panoramic views of the city from the 52nd floor. Award-winning Continental cuisine is served in a warm and elegant atmosphere complemented with masterworks of 18th and 19th century art. Open for dinner nightly from 6 p.m. $$$$

• ***Casablanca***, 101 Main St., Santa Cruz, (408) 426-9063. Gaze out over the sands of Santa Cruz Beach and the ocean as you dine in the casual but elegant atmosphere of Casablanca. The California cuisine is highlighted with outstanding local seafood and fresh ingredients. Open for dinner nightly from 5 p.m. $$

• ***Chez Renee***, 9051 Soquel Dr., Aptos, (408) 688-5566. Tucked away on a quiet street and surrounded by redwoods, this restaurant offers a very comfortable atmosphere. The California cuisine, inspired with a touch of French and Italian, is very good, and the service from the owners makes you feel at home. Open for dinner Tuesday-Saturday. $$$

• ***Cliff House Restaurant***, 1090 Point Lobos, San Francisco, (415) 386-3330. Located in a historic landmark building, the Cliff House is a local favorite that offers a view of the ocean from high atop the cliffs. The seafood/American cuisine is well prepared, and prices are reasonable. Located near Golden Gate Park and Ocean Beach. Open for dinner nightly from 5 p.m. $$$

• ***Dal Baffo***, 878 Santa Cruz Ave., Menlo Park, (415) 325-1588. Laura Ashley fabric walls, white linen, and fine china and crystal set the tone for a romantic interlude. The European/Italian cuisine is incredibly delicious, and service is spectacular. Located in downtown Menlo Park near the beautiful grounds of Stanford University and Stanford Shopping Center. Open for dinner Monday–Saturday from 5 p.m. $$$$

• ***Fleur De Lys***, 777 Sutter St., San Francisco, (415) 673-7779. Well known as one of the most romantic restaurants in San Francisco, Fleur De Lys creates the setting of an immense garden tent set in the French countryside. Their contemporary French cuisine is absolutely fabulous, and the staff attends to your every need. Near the theater district. Open for dinner Monday–Thursday from 6–10 p.m., Friday and Saturday from 5:30– 10:30 p.m. $$$$

• ***Fresh Cream***, 100 C Heritage Harbor, Monterey, (408) 375-9798. This restaurant is probably the most highly recommended in Monterey County. Stunning views of Monterey Bay and elegant decor set the mood for romantic dinners featuring French nouvelle cuisine. Near Fisherman's Wharf. Open for dinner nightly from 6 p.m. $$$$

• ***La Boheme***, Dolores and Seventh Sts., Carmel, (408) 624-7500. This cute little restaurant with warm decor authentically resembles a European cottage. Their three-course prix fixe country French cuisine is well prepared and a good value. Near downtown Carmel and Carmel Beach. Open for dinner nightly from 5:30 p.m. $$$

• ***Le Mouton Noir***, 14560 Big Basin Way, Saratoga, (408) 867-7017. Creative, contemporary California French cuisine is served in this charming 146-year-old Victorian establishment. An outdoor patio and four separate dining areas provide privacy. Located in downtown Saratoga. Open for dinner nightly from 6 p.m. $$$

• ***Old Bath House Restaurant***, 620 Ocean View Blvd., Pacific Grove, (408) 375-5195. Located adjacent to Lover's Point Park, The Old Bath House offers oceanside dining in a romantic atmosphere. Attentive, friendly service, outstanding European cuisine, and the great view make for a wonderful dining experience. Located near downtown Pacific Grove. Open for dinner Monday–Friday from 5–10 p.m., Saturday from 4 p.m. and Sunday from 3 p.m. $$$

• ***Pacific's Edge*** at the Highlands Inn, Hwy. 1, Carmel, (408) 624-0471. Sitting high atop the cliffs, the view of the ocean from a seat at this restaurant is enough to take your breath away. Add fresh and creative menu items, attentive service, and just about any kind of wine to choose from and you are in for a fine dining experience. Open for dinner from 6–10 p.m. $$$$

• ***The Plumed Horse***, 14555 Big Basin Way, Saratoga, (408) 867-4711. All of the elements of a fine romantic restaurant can be found at the Plumed Horse. Outstanding French/Continental cuisine is served in their unique and intimate dining rooms by a very attentive staff. Located in quaint downtown Saratoga. Open for dinner nightly from 6 p.m. $$$

• ***Rue De Paris,*** 19 N. Market St., San Jose, (408) 298-0704. Small and intimate, the finest French cuisine is served in a French country setting away from the hustle and bustle of downtown. Located near the theaters and clubs of San Jose. Open for dinner Monday–Thursday from 5:30–10 p.m. and Friday and Saturday until 11 p.m. $$$

• ***San Benito House*** , 356 Main St., Half Moon Bay, (415) 726-3425. Located in a historic turn-of-the-century hotel, the small San Benito House Restaurant offers gourmet Mediterranean cuisine at a very reasonable price. Everything is homemade and very delicious. Located in downtown Half Moon Bay near the beaches. Open for dinner Thursday–Sunday only from 6.–9p.m. $$

• ***Shadowbrook***, 1750 Wharf Rd., Capitola, (408) 475-1511. Arrive via a quaint cable car tram to a Swiss chalet–style structure that was originally built as a log cabin. Surrounded by award winning gardens and a view of the Soquel Creek, Shadowbrook offers California Continental cuisine at a reasonable price. Near Capitola Village and the beach. Open for dinner Monday–Friday from 5:30–9:30p.m., Saturday and Sunday from 4 p.m. $$

• ***Spadaro's***, 650 Cannery Row, Monterey, (408) 372-8881. Friendly service, a beautiful view of the Monterey Bay, and well prepared Italian cuisine make this the perfect place to go. The atmosphere is relaxing and intimate. Located on historic Cannery Row. Open for dinner nightly from 5 p.m. $$

FAIRS & FESTIVALS

 !! $

Almost every weekend in several places around our region, there are lively fairs and fun festivals taking place. They range in size from small to large, with hundreds to thousands of people taking part. There is no better place to enjoy delicious varieties of food, purchase unique arts and crafts, meet interesting people, and enjoy the charms of the host city.

Walk hand in hand with your date and experience the sights and sounds of these unique gatherings. Buy something nice for your significant other as a memento of your trip. Perhaps a group of friends would like to join you, and afterwards you can all go out for drinks and dinner.

There are hundreds of different festivals and fairs, and we could not list them all. However, the major annual events listed below promise to be especially good.

Forty Five Fun Fairs & Festivals

• ***Clam Chowder Cook-Off***, (408) 423-5590
Santa Cruz Boardwalk, Santa Cruz
February 25, 1995
Every imaginable recipe for clam chowder is served by creatively costumed chefs in a contest at the Boardwalk.

• ***Jazz on the Wharf***, (408) 429-3777
Santa Cruz Municipal Wharf, Santa Cruz

March 12, 1995
Enjoy performances by top jazz musicians among the backdrop of the beach and boardwalk.

• ***Monterey Wine Festival,*** (408) 372-2259
Hyatt Regency Monterey, Monterey
March 23–26, 1995
Join in on the 19th annual celebration of California's best wines at the lovely Hyatt Regency Resort.

• ***Good Old Days Celebration***, (408) 373-3304
Lighthouse Ave., Pacific Grove
April 8–9, 1995
A parade, pie-eating contest, and unique arts & crafts displays help celebrate days gone by in this historic town by the Monterey Bay.

• ***Cherry Blossom Festival***, (415) 563-2313
Japantown, San Francisco
April 14–16 and 21–23, 1995
The arrival of blooming cherry blossoms is celebrated with traditional Japanese fanfare in Japantown.

• ***Pacific Coast Dream Machines***, (415) 726-5067
Half Moon Bay Airport, Half Moon Bay
April 23, 1995
Antique vehicles of all kinds from cars and trucks to airplanes and motorcycles are on display.

• ***Cinco de Mayo Celebration***, (408) 923-1646
Almaden Blvd., San Jose
May 5, 1995
Celebrate Mexico's Independence Day with lively music, costumed dancers, and a parade.

• ***Mayfest Weekend***, (415) 948-1455
Downtown Los Altos

May 20–21, 1995
Four different service organizations put together a celebration that includes a pancake breakfast, fine arts show, and pet parade in this lovely small town.

• ***Carnaval Parade & Festival***, (415) 826-1401
Mission District, San Francisco
May 27–28, 1995
A big parade in the Mission District complete with a combination of floats, bands, Samba groups, belly dancers, and costumed performers.

• ***Pacific Coast Chili & Clam Chowder Cook-off***, (415) 726-9275
Princeton Harbor, Half Moon Bay
June 1995
Enjoy a variety of arts and crafts, live entertainment, country and western dancing, and the chefs' battle for the best chili and clam chowder recipes.

• ***Strawberry Festival***, (408) 379-3790
Civic Center, Los Gatos
June 3–4, 1995
Tasty strawberry sweets, entertainment, and arts and crafts are included in this longtime festival in downtown Los Gatos.

• ***Sunnyvale Art & Wine Festival***, (408) 736-4971
Downtown, Sunnyvale
June 10–11, 1995

• ***Monterey Bay Blues Festival***, (408) 394-2652
Monterey County Fairgrounds, Monterey
June 24–25, 1995
Enjoy the best blues performers all weekend long in this romantic weekend getaway city.

• ***Living History Days,*** (408) 287-2290
San Jose Historical Museum, Kelley Park, San Jose

June 24–25, 1995
Step back in time to the good old days with a parade, an antique car exhibit, and a trolley ride through the park.

• ***Jazz and All That Art on Fillmore***, (415) 346-4446
Fillmore St., San Francisco
July 1–2, 1995
A wide variety of arts and crafts are displayed up and down Fillmore St. among the background sounds of live jazz music.

• ***Fourth of July Waterfront Festival***, (415) 673-3782
Fisherman's Wharf area, San Francisco
July 4, 1995
The largest fireworks extravaganza on the West Coast with live entertainment and 20 minutes of shells launched from three locations along the wharf.

• ***Los Altos Arts & Wine Festival,*** (415) 949-5282
Downtown Los Altos
July 8-9, 1995

• ***California Small Brewers Festival***, (415) 965-2739
Franklin and Evelyn Sts., Mountain View
July 22–23, 1995
After judging a few chili recipes, sample a variety of beers from California's finest small brewers.

• ***Santa Clara County Fair***, (408) 295-3050
Santa Clara County Fairgrounds, San Jose
July 26–August 6, 1995
Enjoy carnival games and rides, a parade, and a host of exhibits.

• ***Gilroy Garlic Festival***, (408) 842-1625
Christmas Hill Park, Gilroy
July 28–30, 1995
A huge celebration of garlic including live entertainment, arts and crafts, and every garlic recipe imaginable (even garlic ice cream!).

• ***Comedy Celebration Day***, (415) 777-8498
Golden Gate Park, San Francisco
July 30, 1995
Comedians from all over the Bay Area give a free performance at the Polo Fields starting at noon.

• ***San Mateo County Fair***, (415) 574-3247
San Mateo County Fairgrounds, San Mateo
August 11–20, 1995
Enjoy a variety of rides, arts and crafts, agricultural exhibits and flower judging.

• ***Cupertino Art & Country Festival***, (408) 252-7054
Cupertino Town Center, Cupertino
August 12-13, 1995

• ***Milpitas Art & Wine Festival***, (408) 262-2613
Milpitas Town Center, Milpitas
August 19-20, 1995

• ***Monterey County Fair***, (408) 372-5863
Monterey County Fairgrounds, Monterey
August 22–27, 1995
This six-day fair includes a variety of agricultural exhibits, arts and crafts, live entertainment, and a carnival.

• ***Victorian Days***, (415) 574-6441
Central Park, San Mateo
August 26–27, 1995
Located downtown in beautiful Central Park, Victorian Days celebrates yesteryear with Civil War reenactments, antique automobiles, and costumed performers.

• ***San Francisco Shakespeare Festival***, (415) 666-2221
Golden Gate Park, San Francisco
August–October 1995

Free Shakespeare performances in the beautiful setting of Golden Gate Park.

• ***Tapestry and Talent Festival of Art,*** (408) 293-9727
Park Ave. and Almaden Blvd., San Jose
September 2–4, 1995
The largest of San Jose's festivals, Tapestry and Talent includes an enormous variety of arts and crafts, live music, and plenty of food.

• ***San Francisco Fair***, (415) 703-2729
Location TBD, San Francisco
September 2–4, 1995
A county fair in the midst of the big city featuring a carnival, live music, and arts and crafts.

• ***Mountain View Art & Wine Festival***, (415) 968-8378
Castro Street, Mountain View
September 9-10, 1995

• ***Santa Cruz County Fair***, (408) 688-3384
Santa Cruz County Fairgrounds, Watsonville
September 12–17, 1995
A wide variety of live entertainment and a host of exhibits.

• ***Monterey Jazz Festival***, (408) 373-3366
Monterey County Fairgrounds, Monterey
September 15–17, 1995
The oldest jazz festival in the world with three days of performances from top jazz musicians.

• ***Santa Clara Art & Wine Festival***, (408) 984-3257
Central Park, Santa Clara
September 16-17, 1995

• ***Art & Wine Festival***, (408) 475-6522
Capitola Village, Capitola
September 16-17, 1995

• ***Pacific Coast Fog Fest***, (415) 355-4122
Palmetto Ave., Pacifica
September 23–24, 1995
Located in the beautiful coastal town of Pacifica, this extremely popular festival features incredible food, arts and crafts, and live entertainment.

• ***San Francisco Blues Festival,*** (415) 826-6837
The Great Meadow at Fort Mason, San Francisco
September 23–24, 1995
Live blues music can be heard all weekend long from the Great Meadow on the northern edge of the Bay.

• ***San Bruno Street Festival***, (415) 588-0180
San Mateo Ave. near El Camino, San Bruno
September 30–October 1, 1995
Little San Bruno puts on a great street festival complete with live music and a large display of arts and crafts.

• ***Festa Italiana***, (415) 673-3782
Fisherman's Wharf area, San Francisco
Late September/Early October 1995
Where better to celebrate an Italian festival than North Beach? Enjoy a variety of Italian cuisine, live entertainment, and bocce ball tournaments.

• ***Pumpkin & Art Festival***, (415) 726-9652
Main St., Half Moon Bay
October 13–15, 1995
As Halloween approaches, come to Half Moon Bay for arts and crafts, a parade, hay rides, and a pumpkin-carving contest.

• ***San Francisco Jazz Festival***, (415) 864-5449
Various locations, San Francisco
October 13–29, 1995

One or two top jazz performances are given at a variety of downtown locations every day.

• ***Butterfly Parade***, (408) 646-6520
Downtown Pacific Grove
October 14, 1995
Celebrate the migration of the monarch butterfly with a parade in this quaint, historic town.

• ***Santa Clara County Holiday Faire***, (408) 295-3050
Santa Clara County Fairgrounds, San Jose
November 18–19 and 25–26, 1995
The holiday season is celebrated with live entertainment, the "Christmas Lane" theme building, and even a visit from Santa Claus.

• ***Christmas Craft Festival***, (408) 423-5590
Cocoanut Grove, Santa Cruz
November 25–26, 1995
Purchase some early Christmas gifts from the numerous artisans displaying their crafts at the beautiful Cocoanut Grove by the beach.

• ***Christmas in the Adobes***, (408) 649-7111
Several locations, Monterey
December 7 and 9, 1995
Monterey's historic adobes are colorfully decorated for a walk-through during the holiday season.

• ***A Victorian Christmas***, (408) 287-2290
San Jose Historical Museum, San Jose
December 9–10, 1995
Come and celebrate an old-fashioned Christmas in this historic "town." Be greeted by costumed performers in Victorian dress, visit colorfully decorated homes, and tell Father Christmas what you want.

HIKING

 !! $

If you are in the mood to escape from the city, then take that special someone hiking and explore the natural beauty around us. Civilization will feel a million miles away, and you will feel better than ever.

Towering waterfalls, majestic redwoods, trickling streams and panoramic views of the coast await you. Being in this kind of environment can clear your mind, relieve you of stress, and help put life back into a simpler perspective. You may also learn a little bit about the thousands of trees and plants crisscrossing our region.

The trails listed below are relatively easy and short, and each offers a unique vista. Go at a comfortable pace and stop and rest when you feel tired. Take a long look around and record your time together with a few pictures.

On your hike, make sure to bring plenty of water to drink to avoid becoming dehydrated. A good pair of climbing shoes, sunglasses, sunscreen, and a compass are not a bad idea either. Most importantly, enjoy your escape into the wilderness.

Ten Scenic Hikes

• Coastal Trail to China Beach

Scenery: Wander along this coastal trail and be rewarded with views of the San Francisco Bay, Golden Gate Bridge, Marin Headlands, Farallon Islands, and Point Reyes.

Directions: From Hwy. 1 north of Santa Cruz, continue on the Great Hwy. (35) until you reach the Cliff House Restaurant (1090 Point Lobos Ave.). The trail starts at the edge of the parking lot (Merrie Way) lying to your left just after the Cliff House.
Distance: 5.0 miles Fee: Free
Contact: Golden Gate National Recreation Area at (415) 556-8371.

• **Fitzgerald Marine Reserve**
Scenery: Enjoy exploring a 30-acre reef containing hundreds of tidepools with small sea creatures everywhere.
Directions: From Hwy. 1 north of Santa Cruz, continue into Moss Beach and turn left onto California St.
Distance: 1.0 mile Fee: Free
Contact: Fitzgerald Marine Reserve at (415) 728-3584.

• **Meteor Trail**
Scenery: Hike along Opal Creek past towering redwoods and come out to the Ocean View Summit, where you will command a view of the coast from 1,600 feet.
Directions: See Redwood Trail directions. Start on the Skyline-to-Sea Trail (northeast), turn left onto Meteor Trail and continue heading towards the ocean. Return the way you came.
Distance: 5.2 miles Fee: $5 day use
Contact: Big Basin Redwoods State Park at (408) 338-6132.

• **Nature Trail to Black Falls**
Scenery: Hike past Swanson Creek and small waterfalls.
Directions: From Hwy. 101 take the Bernal Rd. exit and follow it south to Monterey Hwy. Turn left on Monterey Hwy., right onto Bailey Ave., and left onto McKean Rd. McKean becomes Uvas Rd. Turn right on Croy Rd. and follow it into Uvas Canyon County Park. The trail begins at the Black Oak Group Picnic Area.
Distance: 1.2 miles Fee: $3 day use
Contact: Uvas Canyon County Park at (408) 779-9232.

• **Pfeiffer Falls**
Scenery: This short trail winds down along the Pfeiffer-Redwood Creek, through the redwoods, and up to a 60-foot-high waterfall.
Directions: Travel approximately 27 miles south of Carmel on Hwy. 1 until you reach Pfeiffer Big Sur State Park. Entrance is on your left.
Distance: 1.7 miles Fee: $6 day use
Contact: Pfeiffer Big Sur State Park at (408) 667-2315.

• **Point Lobos State Preserve**
Scenery: Several trails lead you past Monterey cypress trees and ocean coves filled with sea otters, whales, and sea lions. Along the way, you can climb onto several large rock formations and gaze at the Monterey Peninsula.
Directions: From Hwy. 1, head south past Carmel until you reach the entrance to the park on your right.
Distance: Varies depending on the many great trails to choose from. The two best trails, Cypress Grove and Sea Lion Point, are 1.4 miles in length. Fee: $6 day use
Contact: Point Lobos State Reserve at (408) 624-4909.

• **Redwood Trail**
Scenery: See ancient redwoods, including the Santa Clara Tree (17 feet in diameter!), the Father-of-the-Forest tree (2,000 years old), and Mother-of-the-Forest tree (329 feet high), in this popular grove.
Directions: From Hwy. 280., take the Sunnyvale/Saratoga exit and head south until you reach Hwy. 9. Turn right onto Hwy. 9 and follow it over Skyline Ridge until going right onto Hwy. 236. Exit at Big Basin State Park.
Distance: 0.6 mile Fee: $5 day use
Contact: Big Basin Redwoods Sate Park at (408) 338-6132.

• **Ridge Trail to Borel Hill**
Scenery: Climb 250 feet to a large grassland and enjoy a 360-degree view of the San Francisco Peninsula from an elevation of over 2,500 feet!

Directions: From Hwy. 280, take Page Mill Rd. and travel west to Skyline Blvd. Cross Skyline Blvd. and turn into the parking lot on your left. Hike southeast on the Ridge Trail until you reach Borel Hill, a large clearing on your left.
Distance: 1.4 miles Fee: Free
Contact: Midpeninsula Regional Open Space District at (415) 691-1200.

• **Summit Rock**
Scenery: After a short one-mile hike through this mountainous terrain, you will be rewarded with a spectacular view of the Santa Clara Valley.
Directions: From Hwy. 17, get off at the Hwy. 9 exit and follow it through downtown Saratoga and up into the hills until you reach Hwy. 35. Turn south on Hwy. 35 and drive until you reach Sanborn-Skyline Park. The start of the trail is on the left just past the entrance to Castle Rock State Park. Hike north on the Skyline Trail to the Summit Rock Loop.
Distance: 2.0 miles Fee: $3 day use
Contact: Sanborn-Skyline County Park at (408) 867-9959.

• **Sweeney Ridge**
Scenery: Hike along the coast of San Francisco Bay, through the grasslands and wildflowers, to an elevation of 1,200 feet, where you will enjoy commanding views of the South Bay, Pacific Ocean, and a host of mountains.
Directions: From Hwy. 280, take the Westborough exit and proceed west to Hwy. 35. Turn left onto Hwy. 35 and right onto College Drive. Enter Skyline College and park in lot #2. The trail starts off to your right.
Distance: 4.4 miles Fee: Free
Contact: Golden Gate Recreation Area at (415) 556-8371.

Note: There are many great trails located up and down Skyline Blvd. If you are looking to hike several trails in one general area, this is your best bet. Be sure to check out Castle Rock State Park, located on the west side of the road near the Hwy. 9 junction.

HORSEBACK RIDING

 !! $$$

Throw on some jeans, step into your boots, dust off that cowboy hat, and head for a real adventure back in time! The fun all starts with a trip to the stables. We have listed places that are scattered in all sorts of environments from the mountains to the forest to the beach. Each stable is quite rustic, and the people who run them are more than neighborly.

Hop onto that horse and blaze through nature the old-fashioned way. Don't worry if you have never ridden before, as horses for beginners as well as some instruction from the trail boss are available.

One of the best times to travel on horseback is at sunset. Toward the end of your ride, you will be treated to the sight of the sun as it slowly slips under the horizon. As the stars begin to sparkle and the moon starts to glow, a romantic mood will encapture you both. Before you head back to the stables, have one of the trail riders snap a picture among this tranquil backdrop.

This activity gives you the opportunity to explore the outdoors together and learn a little about our surroundings. After the ride, your butt may be a little sore, but you will have memories to treasure forever.

Stables Offering Horseback Riding

• ***Alum Rock Stables***, 16235 Alum Rock Ave., San Jose, (408) 251-8800. Alum Rock Stables has approximately 20 miles of scenic horse trails that extend through the hills and creeks of Alum Rock Park. Their "early bird special" ride ($27.50) starts at 8 a.m. Saturday and Sunday and takes you to Eagle Rock outlook, where you will enjoy a fabulous view of Santa Clara Valley. Open daily from 8 a.m.–4 p.m. $18 per hour or $30 for two hours.

• ***Calero Ranch Stables***, 23201 McKean Rd., San Jose, (408) 268-2567. Fourteen miles of trails in the Calero County Park take you through the hills of San Jose and past the wildlife of the area. Call at least one day in advance for reservations. Open Tuesday–Sunday. $15 per hour or $20 for an hour and a half per rider.

• ***Garrod Farms Stables***, 22600 Mt. Eden Rd., Saratoga, (408) 867-9527. Located just behind the town of Saratoga and connected to the Fremont Older Open Space Preserve, Garrod Farms Stables offers unguided trail rides with spectacular views of the Santa Clara Valley. Open daily from 8:30 a.m.–4:30 p.m. Prices start at $20 per hour per rider.

• ***The Holman Ranch,*** Holman and Carmel Valley Rds., Carmel Valley, (408) 659-2640. A private 400-acre ranch in sun-kissed Carmel Valley. Special rides include a sweetheart trail ride, which is a private, guided one hour trek that includes champagne, chocolates, and a souvenir snapshot ($95 per couple). Open daily by appointment. $30 per hour or $50 for two hours.

• ***MarVista Stables***, 2152 Skyline Blvd., Daly City, (415) 991-4224. Drive along scenic Skyline Blvd. to this ranch that offers a ride down to the beach along San Francisco's western coast. Open daily from 9 a.m.-5 p.m. Prices start at $20 per rider.

• ***Molera Trail Rides***, off Hwy. 1 south of Carmel in Andrew Molera State Park, Big Sur, (408) 625-8664. Seventeen miles of trails wind through the most scenic areas of this 4,800-acre park. During the ride, the trail boss will teach you a little about the surrounding trees, plants, animals, and history of the park. Every ride ends up at the beach, which is most spectacular at sunset. Call ahead for availability. Prices start at $40 per rider.

• ***Pebble Beach Equestrian Center***, Portola and Alva Lane, Pebble Beach, (408) 624-2756. Located in the Del Monte Forest and adjacent to the Lodge at Pebble Beach, they offer 27 miles of trails. A one-and-a-half-hour trail ride takes you through the forest, over the sand dunes, and down to the beach before returning along the world-famous Spyglass Hill golf course. Open daily. Prices start at $30 for a forest ride.

• ***Sea Horse & Friendly Acres Ranch,*** 1828 Cabrillo Hwy. (Hwy. 1.), Half Moon Bay, (415) 726-2362. A combined 25 acres of scenic coastal trails, including a trot on the beach. A two-hour beach ride is only $40. Open daily from 8 a..m.–dusk. Cost is $22 per hour for trail rides.

"When love is good it can make you fly. Winning it is worth the risk. People fall in love and glow for weeks."

George Davis

HOT AIR BALLOONING

!!!! $$$$

Hot air ballooning began in France over 200 years ago. Since that first magical flight, many have embarked on a journey that takes you thousands of feet up in a small wicker basket. Drifting across the quiet sky with the glow of the rising sun behind you is a romantic experience not soon forgotten.

There is nothing to be nervous about as these gorgeous balloons, filled with heated air, sweep across the ocean, valleys and mountains of our area. Upon landing, enjoy a special treat of champagne as you celebrate your successful journey in this unique air ship.

Many flights begin in the early morning due to calm weather conditions. Afterward, go wine tasting, horseback riding, kayaking, or take a scenic drive over the land you just flew over. If you embark on a sunset ride, extend your evening at a local bed & breakfast and enjoy sharing your adventure over a romantic dinner.

Hot Air Ballooning

• ***Balloons by the Sea***, Salinas, (408) 424-0111. Hot air balloon rides Monterey style, with views of the Salinas Valley and Monterey Peninsula. Sunrise flights scheduled daily all year, and sunset flights offered in fall and winter. Cost of $155 per person includes champagne celebration and framed flight certificate.

• ***Balloons Espirit***, Half Moon Bay, (415) 726-6006. A small ballooning company that offers very personalized service, as only the pilot and one couple go up each day. One flight per day in the early morning. Basic packages start at $250 per couple.

• ***Balloons for Higher***, Los Gatos, (408) 358-0043. Small ballooning company utilizing independent commercial balloonists who fly over the South Bay Wine Country. Balloon flights seven days a week at various times. Cost of $140 per person includes a champagne brunch and flight certificate.

• ***The Gentle Adventure***, Morgan Hill, (408) 778-1945. Drift over a valley covered with orchards and vineyards in the South Bay wine country. One flight per day takes place just after dawn. Cost of $140 per adult includes champagne ceremony with diploma and a picnic or brunch.

• ***Note***: There are many balloon companies located north of us in Sonoma and Napa Valley, just one hour from San Francisco. If you are willing to make the trip, try calling one of the following: Air Flamboyant (707-575-1989), Balloon Aviation (707) 944-4400, and Once in a Lifetime (707) 578-0580.

ICE & ROLLER SKATING

!! $

Most people get their first taste of skating at an early age. To make it once around the rink without falling is a major accomplishment. In time, you learn how to speed around the rink, jumping and spinning and having a lot of fun.

Although outdoor rollerblading is one of the more popular activities today, there are still plenty of people coming to the ice and roller rinks in the area. One reason why is because it is the one place you can skate on a smooth surface, skate to music, and meet a lot of other skaters.

If you have mastered roller skating, try ice skating, and vice versa. Maybe after some practice, you will dazzle your date with a double toe loop or by skating backward. Whatever your skill, just holding hands while taking a few turns around the rink is fun and romantic.

Ice Rinks

•***Belmont Iceland***, 815 Old County Rd., Belmont, (415) 592-0532. Admission: $5.50. Rentals: $2.

•***Eastridge Ice Arena***, 2190-A Tully Rd., San Jose, (408) 238-0440. Admission: $5. Rentals: $2.

•***Golden Gate Ice Arena***, 3140 Bay Rd., Redwood City, (415) 364-8090. Admission: $6. Rentals: $2.

•***Ice Capades Chalet***, 10123 N. Wolfe Rd., Cupertino, (408) 446-2906. Admission: $5. Rentals: $2

•***Ice Centre of San Jose***, 1500 S. 10th St., San Jose, (408) 279-6000. Admission: $5.50. Rentals: $2.50

•***Ice Chalet***, 2202 San Mateo Fashion Island, San Mateo, (415) 574-1616. Admission: $5. Rentals: $2.

•***The Winter Lodge***, 3009 Middlefield Rd., Palo Alto, (415) 493-4566. Admission: $5. Rentals: $2.

<u>Roller Rinks</u>

•***Cal Skate of Milpitas***, 980 Los Cochas, Milpitas, (408) 946-1363. Admission: $4. Rentals included.

•***Del Monte Gardens***, Del Monte Blvd., Monterey, (408) 375-3202. Admission: $4. Rentals included.

•***Golden Skate Center***, 397 Blossom Hill Rd., San Jose, (408) 226-1156. Admission: $4.50 (day), $4.75 (evenings). Rentals included.

•***The Rink***, 251 Kings Village Rd., Scotts Valley, (408) 438-2222. Admission: Varies. Rentals included.

•***Rolladium Roller Rink***, 363 N. Amphlett, San Mateo, (415) 342-2711. Admission: $4.50. Rentals included.

•***Santa Cruz Roller Paladium,*** 1606 Seabright, Santa Cruz, (408) 423-0844. Admission: $3.35 (day), $4.50 (evenings). Rentals included.

•***Skateworld Roller Rink***, 3667 Stevens Creek Blvd., Santa Clara, (408) 247-7772. Admission: $4. Rentals included.

KAYAKING

♡♡ !!! $$

Kayaking is one of the fastest growing recreational activities today. It is relaxing, fun, easy to learn, and available in a variety of locations from the marine sanctuary of Monterey Bay to the beaches of Santa Cruz. Wherever you launch from, kayaking offers a unique view of marine life and our spectacular coastline.

Kayaks are quiet, simple, highly efficient, and great fun to paddle. Lessons for beginners who want to venture out on easy waters can take just minutes. In no time, you will develop a steady stroke and start exploring the natural wonders of the ocean.

When you are ready to progress, some of the shops listed below offer guided tours and multiple-day trips out of the area in more challenging waters. Another option is to just take it easy and let them take care of you. Adventures by the Sea in Monterey will even deliver a picnic lunch to you at the beach at Lovers Point.

Kayak Rentals & Tours

• ***Adventures by the Sea***, 299 Cannery Row, Monterey, (408) 372-1807. Rent an open kayak and paddle from Lover's Point to Fisherman's Wharf. Enjoy beautiful views of the Monterey Peninsula and observe otters, sea lions, and harbor seals up close.

Costs: rentals ($25 all day), tours ($45). Open daily from 9 a.m.–5 p.m.

• ***Adventure Sports Unlimited***, 303 Potrero St., #15, Santa Cruz, (408) 458-3648. With close access to the ocean, sloughs, reservoirs, and rivers, kayak rentals can be taken most anywhere, including the Santa Cruz Beach & Boardwalk. Costs: rentals ($25 per day). Call for availability.

• ***California Canoe and Kayak***, 214 Princeton Ave., Princeton by the Sea, (415) 728-1803. Specializing in sea kayaking at this store location, different classes include a lesson for beginners, a four-mile Bay-crossing trek, and an introduction to paddling in rougher waters. Multiple-day trips from places like Sacramento and Baja California are also offered. Costs: rentals ($30 all day), classes ($65–$180) and trips ($79–$1,325). Rentals and classes offered all year round. Call for availability.

• ***Kayak Connection***, 413 Lake Ave., Santa Cruz, (408) 479-1121, and 2370 Hwy. 1, Moss Landing, (408) 724-5692. Paddle out onto the open ocean along the Santa Cruz Boardwalk or through the marshlands of Elkhorn Slough, where you will find hundreds of species of birds and fish. Both locations offer kayak rentals, guided tours, and classes. Costs: rentals ($27-$32 half day), tours and classes ($35). Open Tuesday–Friday from 10 a.m.–5 p.m., Saturday and Sunday from 8:30 a.m.–5 p.m.

• ***Monterey Bay Kayaks***, 693 Del Monte Ave., Monterey, (408) 373-KELP. They offer classes, guided tours, and rentals of sea kayaks for tours of the Monterey Bay in both closed and open kayaks. Costs: rentals ($20 all day), guided tours ($48–$55), and classes ($70–$115). Call for availability.

KIDS FOR A DAY

♡ !! $

Many of us have wonderful memories of our childhood. Although we did not have all of the rights of an adult, we did not have all of the responsibilities that now face us either. Without worrying about taxes, jobs, and monthly bills, we as children could go out and just have fun.

Sometimes we would like to go back to those carefree days. Listed below are a few ideas for things to do in the area that might bring back some of those fond memories of yesteryear. Maybe you are originally from this area, and your date would enjoy seeing where you grew up.

For at least one day, set aside your worries and enjoy being kids again.

Fifteen Ways to Feel Like a Kid Again

☺ Go to a neighborhood park and sit on the swings.

☺ Ride the roller coasters and play the carnival games at an amusement park.

☺ Watch a children's performance at the children's theater or at an elementary or middle school.

☺ Sit in the stands at a Little League baseball game, soccer game, or Pop Warner football game.

- ☺ Eat out at a restaurant like Chuck E Cheese where the emphasis is on fun and games.
- ☺ Visit the animals at the San Francisco Zoo and learn a little more about them.
- ☺ Ride the miniature Billy Jones Wildcat Railroad from Oak Meadow Park in Los Gatos to Vasona Park.
- ☺ Play a round of miniature golf.
- ☺ Go to a toy store and buy a fun game to play at home.
- ☺ Rent an animated film like *Aladdin* or *Beauty and the Beast.*
- ☺ Get up early on a Saturday, watch cartoons, and eat sugary cereal.
- ☺ Spend a few dollars playing games at a local arcade center.
- ☺ Go ice skating or roller skating.
- ☺ Go to Baskin Robbins and get three fun flavors stacked up high on top of a sugar cone.
- ☺ Play a high-tech game of cops and robbers at a paint ball or Lazer tag game center.

Limousine Tours

♡♡♡ !! $$$$

There are so many places you can travel in style in a beautiful stretch limousine. So why is it that we are usually seen in them only on our way to a wedding, to a prom, or to the airport?

Live a little and plan a special day with one of the limousine companies listed below. Whether you are interested in touring the local wine country, going to Napa or Monterey, or cruising the dance clubs of San Francisco, they will take care of every detail. You will not have to worry about mapping out your trip, driving, or the hassles of parking.

Limousines are not for only the rich and famous. Hourly rates begin at only $39, and many companies throw in a bottle of bubbly and a few other extras. All you have to do is sit back, relax, and enjoy your adventure in comfort.

Note: There is a 3 hour minimum for most limousine rentals.

Limousine Tour Companies

• ***Bungay's Celebrity Limousine***, Carmel, (408) 624-1407. Local service has been offered for over 10 years to customers on the Monterey Peninsula. Rates from $40 per hour. Favorite routes: 17-mile drive and south along Hwy. 1 to Hearst Castle and Santa Barbara; Four-hour wine tour along with box lunch and champagne.

• ***Chauffeured Limousines***, San Mateo, (415) 344-4400. Large fleet of sedans, and stretch and superstretch vehicles. Rates from $45 per hour. Favorite routes: Hwy. 101 to Sausalito through Muir Woods to the wine country, Hwy. 17 through Santa Cruz and on to Monterey/Carmel.

• ***Chic Limousine***, Sunnyvale, (408) 736-5555. Tuxedoed chauffeurs take you anywhere in the Bay Area. Rates from $39 per hour including champagne, keepsake photo, long-stem roses, and a balloon bouquet. Favorite tours: Napa Valley for wine tasting and ballooning, Monterey for a romantic dinner and the beach, night on the town in San Francisco and dinner cruise on the Bay.

• ***Club Limo***, Santa Cruz, (408) 464-2600. Besides the regular limousine cars, they also have a Corvette limo available for $75 per hour. They do not have any dedicated tour routes, but they know the area well and can take you to the best spots starting for $50 per hour including champagne.

• ***Expresso Limousine Service***, Los Gatos and San Jose, (408) 356-3255 or (408) 293-5466. Twenty different packages ranging in cost from as little as $60. Favorite tours: Napa Valley winery tour, picnic on the Green, Carmel by the Sea, Santa Clara Valley wine tours.

• ***Gateway Limousine***, Burlingame, (415) 697-5548. Serving the entire Peninsula, including the northern coast, they offer a ride in 6, 8 and 10 passenger stretch limousines, sedans, and classic Rolls Royces. Rates from $45 per hour. Favorite routes include Monterey/Carmel, Muir Woods, San Francisco skyline and clubs.

• ***Uptown Limousine***, San Francisco, (415) 589-7373. Uptown Limousine has a modern fleet of luxury sedans and stretch limousines. Prices start at $45 per hour. Favorite tours include San Francisco, the wine country, Monterey/Carmel, and Yosemite.

MINIATURE GOLF

♡ !! $

Miniature golf is not just for kids. It is a serious sport that involves great athletic ability, keenness of mind and hours of practice. It is not just a game; it is a miniature adventure.

All kidding aside, you can have a good time playing 18 holes on a carpeted course dotted with windmills and water traps. The game does take a little hand-to-eye coordination and a whole lot of patience. Every course seems to have a few holes where you have to hit it just right or suffer taking a score of "6." However, you can usually walk off the course with your pride intact and even a free game if you hit it straight on the 19th hole.

You can spend hours playing golf, arcade games, and eating your share of junk food. It is an inexpensive date and a good way to get to know someone better.

Miniature Golf Courses

• ***Buccaneer Bay Miniature Golf*** at Santa Cruz Beach Boardwalk, 400 Beach St., Santa Cruz (408) 423-5590. Features two story, 18-hole indoor course, arcade, and food service. Call for days and hours open (limited during fall and winter). Cost is $5 per person per round.

• ***Golfland***, 1199 Jacklin Rd., Milpitas, (408) 263-3734. Features 18-hole course, arcade, and food service. Open Sunday–Thursday from 10 a.m.–11 p.m. and Friday and Saturday from 10 a.m.–midnight. Cost is $5 per person per round.

• ***Golfland***, 976 Blossom Hill Rd., San Jose, (408) 255-1533. Features two 18-hole courses, arcade, food service, and water slides (summer only). Open Sunday–Thursday from 10 a.m.–10 p.m. and Friday and Saturday from 10 a.m.–midnight. Cost is $5 per person per round.

• ***Golfland***, 855 E. El Camino Real, Sunnyvale, (408) 245-8434. Features two 18-hole courses, arcade, and food service. Open Sunday–Thursday from 10 a.m.–11 p.m. and Friday and Saturday from 10 a.m.–midnight. Cost is $5 per person per round.

• ***Malibu Castle Golf & Games***, 320 Blomquist, Redwood City, (415) 367-1906. Features three-18 hole courses, arcade, food service, batting cages, and sprint car track. Open weekdays from 10 a.m.–midnight, Saturday & Sunday starting at 9 a.m. Cost is $5.95 per person per round.

MOVIES

At one time or another, everyone has taken a date to the movies or rented a film to watch together. For a few hours you have the chance to get wrapped up in a screenwriter's vision of reality, eat popcorn, and hold your date's hand. At the end of the movie, you can go out for drinks, coffee or take a nice scenic drive and talk.

If you are interested in a flashback to the past, go to a drive-in movie theater. The two of you can snuggle together in the comfort of your own private theater seats. There are only a few of these theaters left, so get there while you can.

With the popularity of movie rentals booming over the past few years, you will not be hard pressed to find a rental store like Blockbuster somewhere nearby. They should carry many of the romantic comedies and dramas listed below.

Twenty Five Top Movies with Romance

- *The Accidental Tourist* (1988) William Hurt/ Geena Davis
- *The Apartment* (1960) Jack Lemmon/ Shirley MacLaine
- *Arthur* (1981) Dudley Moore/ Liza Minnelli
- *Beauty and the Beast* (1991) animated
- *Breakfast at Tiffany's* (1961) Audrey Hepburn/ George Pappard
- *Bull Durham* (1988) Kevin Costner/ Susan Sarandon

- *Casablanca* (1942) Humphrey Bogart/ Ingrid Bergman
- *Children of a Lesser God* (1986) William Hurt/ Marlee Matlin
- *Crocodile Dundee* (1986) Paul Hogan/ Linda Kozlowski
- *The French Lieutenant's Woman* (1981) Meryl Streep/ J. Irons
- *From Here to Eternity* (1953) Burt Lancaster/ Deborah Kerr
- *Ghost* (1990) Patrick Swayze/ Demi Moore
- *Gone with the Wind* (1939) Clark Gable/ Vivien Leigh
- *The Long, Hot Summer* (1958) Paul Newman/ J. Woodward
- *Love Affair* (1994) Warren Beatty/Annette Bening
- *Manhattan* (1979) Woody Allen/ Diane Keaton
- *Moonstruck* (1987) Cher/ Nicolas Cage
- *An Officer and a Gentleman* (1982) Richard Gere/ Debra Winger
- *Pretty Woman* (1990) Richard Gere/ Julia Roberts
- *Romancing the Stone* (1984) Michael Douglas/ Kathleen Turner
- *Roxanne* (1987) Steve Martin/ Daryl Hannah
- *Same Time, Next Year* (1978) Alan Alda/ Ellen Burstyn
- *Sleepless in Seattle* (1993) Tom Hanks/ Meg Ryan
- *The Way We Were* (1973) Barbara Streisand/ Robert Redford
- *When Harry Met Sally* (1989) Billy Crystal/ Meg Ryan

Drive-In Theaters

• ***Capitol Drive-In***, Capitol Expwy. and Monterey Rd., San Jose, (408) 226-2251.

• ***Geneva Drive-In***, 607 Carter, Daly City, (415) 587-2884.

• ***Peninsula Drive-In Theater***, 350 Beach Rd., Burlingame, (415) 343-2213.

• ***Skyview Drive-In***, Soquel Dr. and Hwy. 1, Santa Cruz, (408) 475-3405.

MURDER MYSTERY THEATER

 !! $$$

Take some fine actors and actresses, throw in a murder plot, a well-prepared meal, and a little wine and voila—murder mystery dinner theater. It is unlike any other dining experience you have ever had.

Instead of just the two of you, there are several couples, a small stage, and a troupe of performers. For a couple of hours you are provided with clues that you must put together to solve the crime. By the time dessert is finished, everyone submits their best guess, and the murderer is identified.

As you are being entertained by such productions as "Airship of Fools," "Cafe Noir," and "Til Death Do Us Part," you will dine on marvelous cuisine. Since most plays take place in between courses, your meal will not be disturbed.

Dinner Theaters

• ***A. Sabella's Restaurant***, Fisherman's Wharf, 2766 Taylor St., San Francisco, (415) 991-CLUE. Entree to Murder features a four-act play, and A. Sabella's provides a delicious three-course meal. Cost: $45 per person. Shows Friday and Saturday at 8 p.m.

• ***Mac's Tea Room***, 325 Main St., Los Altos, (415) 941-0234. Throughout the evening you will meet a host of intriguing characters and get a chance to question them to find out who the murderer is. Cost: $84 per couple includes a four-course dinner. Shows take place Saturday at 7:30 p.m. Please make reservations at least one week in advance.

• ***The Mansions Hotel & Restaurant***, 2220 Sacramento St., San Francisco, (415) 929-9444. Tour San Francisco's Haunted Mansions and enjoy performances by world-class magicians. Cost: $40. Performances Friday and Saturday. (Not murder mystery but a magical performance nonetheless)

• ***Murder on the Menu***, shows at various locations, (510) 339-2800. Their interactive murder mysteries include 1920s Gangster, 1940s Radio Mystery, and a 1950s High School Reunion play. Contact their office for information on where public performances are taking place.

• ***Pacific Fresh Restaurant***, 1130 N. Mathilda, Sunnyvale, (408) 745-1710. A 3 hour interactive murder mystery takes place all around you as you dine. Cost: $34–$42 per person includes dinner. Shows take place Friday at 7:15 p.m. and Saturday at 6:45 p.m. Please make reservations two to five days in advance.

PERFORMING ARTS

♡♡ !! $$$

In the romantic comedy *Pretty Woman*, Edward (Richard Gere) surprises Vivian (Julia Roberts) with a trip to San Francisco on a private plane to see an opera. Vivian, dressed in a beautiful red gown, and Edward, outfitted in a black tuxedo, enjoy a magical and emotional night at the opera.

Going to the opera, theater, ballet, or symphony does not have to be formal or even expensive. Unlike the days of old, people enjoy performances dressed in anything from formal wear to casual clothing and tickets can costs less than $10 each.

The performing arts have different forms of entertainment to match the tastes of most anyone. The one thing all performances have in common is great music. There are the commanding roar of a tenor, the calming sounds of the strings, the powerful crescendos of the horns, and the vibrant scores of a musical. Anyone with a real appreciation for music will enjoy themselves.

If you have the means, arrive first class to an evening performance in a stretch limousine with champagne on ice. Have two tickets in hand for front orchestra or balcony seating. Whatever you can afford, make it an evening to remember.

Opera

• ***Opera San Jose***, Montgomery Theater, Market and San Carlos Sts., San Jose, (408) 283-4880. 1994–1995 performances (all with supertitles) include favorites like *Carmen* and *La traviata.* Opera season runs from September–May. Series ticket prices range from $20–$35 per performance.

• ***San Francisco Opera***, War Memorial Opera House, 301 Van Ness Ave. at Grove, San Francisco, (415) 864-3330. Ranked as one of the top opera companies in the world, the San Francisco Opera performances take place in the beautiful 3,000-seat War Memorial Opera House. Opera season runs from September–December. Ticket prices range from $20–$120.

• ***West Bay Opera Guild***, Lucie Stern Theater, Middlefield at Melville, Palo Alto, (415) 321-3471. Now in their 39th season, the West Bay Opera Guild presents three operas, including *La Boheme*. Performances in October, February, May, and June. Cost is $80 for a season subscription.

Symphony

• ***Monterey County Symphony***, Sunset Theater (Carmel) and Sherwood Hall (Salinas), (408) 624-8511. Director Clark Suttle celebrates his 10th anniversary season with six wonderful performances. Concerts take place from October–May. Ticket prices start at $10.

• ***Peninsula Symphony***, performances at a variety of locations from Cupertino to San Mateo, (415) 574-0244. Now in their 46th season, the Peninsula Symphony offers four concerts and several "extras," including a holiday concert and a free Summer Pops concert in July. Performances from October–July. Series tickets range from $25–$30.

• ***San Francisco Symphony***, Davies Symphony Hall, Van Ness Ave. at Grove, San Francisco, (415) 431-5400. This well renowned symphony offers special event performances during the holidays, a Summer Pops series, as well as favorite musical scores by Beethoven and Tchaikovsky. The performance season runs from September–July. Ticket prices range from $9–$65.

• ***San Jose Symphony***, Center for the Performing Arts, Flint Center and San Jose State Event Center, (408) 288-2828. The San Jose Symphony performs over 60 concerts a year, including holiday concerts, SuperPops!, and KickBack Classics. Performances take place from September–June (some summer concerts may be added). Tickets range from $10.50–$65.50.

• ***Santa Cruz County Symphony***, Santa Cruz Civic Auditorium, 307 Church St. at Center St., Santa Cruz, (408) 429-3444. John Larry Granger leads the symphony in six outstanding programs celebrating mankind's victory over adversity. Concert season runs from September–May. A free Pops for Pops concert is scheduled on Father's Day at Henry Cowell Redwoods State Park. Season subscription rates range from $16.50–$25 per performance.

Ballet

• ***San Francisco Ballet***, War Memorial Opera House, 301 Van Ness Ave. at Grove, San Francisco, (415) 861-1177. Nationally recognized performances including such favorites as *The Nutcracker*, *Romeo and Juliet*, and *The Sleeping Beauty*. Special performance series tickets can be purchased for ballets taking place from February 7–May 14. Ticket prices are $21–$240 for three performances, $35–$400 for five performances, and $56–$640 for eight performances.

• ***San Jose Cleveland Ballet***, San Jose Center for the Performing Arts, Almaden Blvd. and Woz Way, San Jose, (408) 288-2800. Perhaps not as well known as the San Francisco Ballet, but they rank among the top 10 ballet companies in the United States! Performances run from September–April, and this season concludes with *Romeo and Juliet* in April. Ticket prices range from $13–$50.

Major Theater Performances

• ***Club Fugazi***, 678 Green St. at Powell, San Francisco, (415) 421-4222. *Beach Blanket Babylon*, the longest running musical revue is performed here every Wednesday–Sunday. In the confines of this comfortable club, enjoy a glass of champagne and the zany performances of celebrity lookalikes.

• ***Curran Theater***, 445 Geary St. at Mason, San Francisco, (415) 776-1999. *The Phantom of the Opera* is running through June 1995 at this historic theater that plays host to a variety of popular plays and musicals.

• ***Flint Center***, De Anza College, 21250 Stevens Creek Blvd., Cupertino, (408) 998-2277. The Flint Center hosts a variety of events, including plays, the symphony, and even special appearances by the likes of David Copperfield and Florence Henderson. Events take place at the Flint Center all year round. Call for ticket prices.

• ***Golden Gate Theater***, One Taylor St. at Golden Gate and Market, San Francisco, (415) 776-1999. Fully restored to its original grandeur, the Golden Gate Theater opened the new year with the sensational musical *Grease*.

• ***Marines Memorial Theater***, 609 Sutter St. at Mason, San Francisco, (415) 771-6900. They continue to consistently bring hit after hit to their stage, including the widely popular *Angels in America*.

• ***Peninsula Civic Light Opera***, San Mateo Performing Arts Center, Delaware St., San Mateo, (415) 579-5568. After a terrific season last year, the Peninsula Civic Light Opera will present another three great musicals, including *Will Rogers Follies* and *Meet Me in St. Louis*. Performances April–May, July, and September–October. Tickets are $40 for the season ($18 for individual performances).

• ***San Jose Civic Light Opera***, San Jose Center for the Performing Arts, Almaden Blvd. and Woz Way, San Jose, (408) 453-7108. *42nd Street* and *A Chorus Line* are part of a wonderful selection of musicals for the 1995 season. Ticket prices for three musicals range from $10–$37 each.

• ***San Jose Repertory Theater***, Montgomery Theater (S. Market and W. San Carlos Sts., San Jose) and Mayer Theater (Santa Clara University), (408) 291-2255. Now in their 15th season, the San Jose Repertory Theater produces their own shows, including musicals, dramas, and mysteries. The season runs from October–July. Tickets range from $12–24.

• ***San Jose Stage Company***, 490 S. First St., San Jose, (408) 283-7142. They feature premiere plays and fresh interpretations of popular classics like *Cat on a Hot Tin Roof,* and *A Christmas Carol.* Performances from October–June. Call for ticket prices.

• ***Theater on the Square***, 450 Post St. at Powell, San Francisco, (415) 433-9500. Enjoy a variety of Broadway shows and local talent from a seat in this elegant club. Recent performances included the heralded musical revue *Forever Tango.*

• ***TheaterWorks,*** performances at The Mountain View Center for the Performing Arts (Mountain View) and Lucie Stern Theater (Palo Alto), (415) 903-6000. Now in their 25th anniversary season, TheaterWorks presents ten full productions each year that are innovative and culturally diverse. Call for ticket prices.

SPECIAL OCCASION DATES

✓Carriage ride
✓Chartered sunset cruise
✓Dining in
✓Dining out
✓Hot air ballooning
✓Limousine tour
✓Performing arts
✓Romancing Monterey
✓Romantic getaway
✓San Francisco adventure

PHYSICAL ACTIVITIES

 !! $

Unless you are following a strict exercise routine at the gym, chances are you get caught up in the vicious cycle of the work-home-television-sleep routine. After a while, you begin to run out of steam, and it becomes harder and harder to muster any energy. It is time to get out of the house and get your heart pumping again.

The sports listed below are perfect for two people, and they do not cost a lot of money. You can enjoy most of these activities at your local sports or recreation center. For further information on the recreation center nearest you, consult your phone book.

Note: With every activity, make sure you are physically fit enough to safely participate.

Sporting Activities

☆ ***Basketball***: Shoot a few hoops and play a game of "H-O-R-S-E" at a neighborhood school, park, or recreation center.

☆ ***Bicycling***: Take a short ride around the neighborhood, down to a local park, or explore one of the bicycle adventures detailed on pages 17-22.

☆ ***Bowling***: Bowling alleys are not the most glamorous places to spend time, but you can have a great time there. Make sure to avoid league nights because you may not find an open lane.

☆ ***Golf***: Great courses of all difficulties can be found in our region. Monterey County alone has 18, including the famed Pebble Beach and Spyglass courses. Costs at various courses range from as little as $10 per round at twilight to $225 per round at the best courses. For less money, you can spend an hour hitting balls at the driving range.

☆ ***Jogging***: If you do not have a lot of time, run around the track at a local school. Otherwise, run on an uncrowded scenic path.

☆ ***Racquetball***: If you are in good shape and in the mood for a real workout, go down to your neighborhood park or local sports center and play a game of racquetball.

☆ ***Skating***: Get out your rollerblades and hit the nearest scenic trail or head for the neighborhood rink.

☆ ***Swimming***: Swim a few laps or just enjoy the water.

☆ ***Tennis***: Play a casual game of tennis at a neighborhood park or tennis center or get more involved and take lessons together.

PICNICS

♡♡♡ ! $

In the midst of one of the most populated areas in the country, there exist some beautiful, spacious, and quiet parks in every neighborhood. You may already have a favorite spot to picnic nearby, but we suggest going on a little adventure.

Listed below are some of the best neighborhood parks in our region. Gather together your picnic basket and blanket, hop in the car, and visit a picnicker's paradise outside your local community. Enjoy a leisurely drive and look forward to investigating a new area.

So what food do you put in that picnic basket? Here are a few suggestions:

✎ Crackers

✎ Imported cheese

✎ Sourdough bread or croissants

✎ Fresh fruit (strawberries, grapes, and apples are nice)

✎ Sliced deli meats

✎ Something to barbecue. All of the parks listed below have grills in the designated picnic areas. Marinated chicken breasts or hamburgers are good choices for the barbecue.

✎ Fresh vegetables and dip

✎ Beverage: A nice Chardonnay goes well with everything in a picnic basket. Most parks allow alcohol as long as you are in the picnic grounds and over the age of 21. Otherwise, try sparkling cider, mineral water, or soda.

Find a quiet spot with a view, lay down your blanket or sit at a picnic table, and enjoy a great meal outdoors.

Ten Beautiful Parks

• ***Central Park***, 50 E. 5th at El Camino, San Mateo, (415) 377-4700. Walk through this 18-acre park and enjoy serene Japanese and rose gardens. Near downtown San Mateo. No fee.

• ***Central Park***, 969 Kiely near Homestead, Santa Clara, (408) 984-3257. A wide pathway leads you through this 52-acre park that includes a beautiful lake with fountain, small waterfall, and a large picnic area. Adjacent to community center. No fee.

• ***Community Park***, Edmundson Ave. near Monterey Rd., Morgan Hill, (408) 779-7283. 23-acre park situated around a large duck pond and bordered by golden, cow-studded hills. Near downtown Morgan Hill. No fee.

• ***Coyote Point County Recreation Area***, Coyote Point Dr. and N. Bayshore Blvd., San Mateo, (415) 573-2592. Bordering the San Francisco Bay, Coyote Point includes a marina, museum, wildlife habitats, yacht club, picnic areas, beach access, and the Castaway Restaurant. Great view of the boats on the bay and the airplanes landing at San Francisco International Airport. Entrance fee of $4 per car.

• ***Cuesta Park***, 685 Cuesta Ave. at Grant Rd., Mountain View, (415) 903-6331. Very quiet 33-acre park with rolling grassy knolls and plenty of shade trees to relax under. Near shopping and restaurants on El Camino Real. No fee.

• ***El Estero Park***, Camino el Estero and Fremont Blvd., Monterey (408) 646-3866. Lake El Estero sits in the center of this 45-acre park that includes walking trails, paddleboat rentals, and the Dennis the Menace playground. Near downtown Monterey, Fisherman's Wharf, and Monterey State Beach. No fee.

• ***Golden Gate Park***, bordered by Fulton St., Lincoln Way, Stanyan St. and the Great Highway, San Francisco, (415) 666-7200. This 1,017-acre park includes grassy picnic areas, wooded walking trails, several lakes, and scenic bike routes. Attractions inside the park include the California Academy of Sciences, deYoung Museum, Asian Art Museum, Japanese Tea Garden, Conservatory of Flowers, Strybing Arboretum and Botanical Gardens, and the Shakespeare Garden. The park is located near Ocean Beach and the San Francisco Zoo. No entry fee but each activity will cost you a few dollars.

• ***Henry Cowell Redwoods State Park***, Highway 9 one mile south of Felton, Santa Cruz, (408) 335-4598. This 1,737-acre redwood park features miles of trails, a nature center and a picnic area above the San Lorenzo River. Day use fee of $5.

• ***Lover's Point Park,*** Ocean View Blvd., Pacific Grove, (408) 373-3304. A small park and beach offering a lovely view across the ocean of the Monterey Peninsula. Near quaint town of Pacific Grove, Cannery Row, and scenic Ocean View Blvd. No fee.

• ***Vasona Park***, Blossom Hill and Garden Hill Dr., Los Gatos, (408) 356-2729. This 151-acre park, centered around Lake Vasona, offers several different picnic grounds, boat rentals, and bicycle and walking trails. The Billy Jones Wildcat Railroad will take you around the grounds and to neighboring ***Oak Meadow Park***. Near downtown Los Gatos. Entry fee collected.

BEST OUTDOOR DATES

✓Beach
✓Bicycle adventures
✓Cruising the Pacific
✓Fairs & Festivals
✓Hiking
✓Horseback riding
✓Kayaking
✓Physical Activites
✓Picnics
✓Whale watching

PRO SPORTING EVENTS

♡ !!! $$$

This area is blessed with talented professional sports teams. In football, we have a world championship team with the best record over the last 10 years. In baseball, the Athletics and Giants are always competitive, and both teams have recently been to the World Series. Our new hockey team, the San Jose Sharks, surprised everyone last season with their first playoff appearance. The Golden State Warriors, barring the loss of any more star players, could be playoff bound again in no time.

You can watch a game on television, or you can go to the game and be a part of the whole experience. The first time that baseball diamond or basketball court comes into view, you can start to feel the excitement. Watching some of your favorite athletes doing incredible things on the field of play cannot be replaced by seeing it on television.

Get to the games early. Get some autographs, purchase a souvenir, and visit the concession stands for a beverage and hot dog. Yell, scream, and shout, and when the game begins have fun sharing this experience with your date.

Regional Sports Teams

• ***Golden State Warriors,*** Oakland-Alameda County Coliseum Complex at Interstate 880 and Hegenberger Rd., Oakland, (510) 569-2121. The Warriors lost in the first round of the NBA playoffs in 1993-1994, but strive to improve with newly acquired talent. Basketball season runs from November–April.

• ***Oakland Athletics***, Oakland-Alameda County Coliseum Complex, Interstate 880 and Hegenberger Rd., Oakland, (510) 569-2121. The Athletics were playing well and climbing toward the top of the division when the strike happened. Baseball season runs from April–October.

• ***San Francisco Forty-Niners,*** Candlestick Park at Giants Dr. and Gilman Ave., San Francisco, (415) 468-2249. The Niners went to the Superbowl during the 1994 season, and are consistently amongst the top teams in the NFL. Football season runs from August–January.

• ***San Francisco Giants,*** Candlestick Park at Giants Dr. and Gilman Ave., San Francisco, (415) 467-8000. During the strike shortened 1994 season, the Giants finished in second place. Baseball season runs from April–October.

• ***San Jose Sharks***, San Jose Arena at W. Santa Clara and Autumn Sts., San Jose, (408) 287-9200. During the 1993–1994 season, the Sharks surprised many by making it to the semi-finals of the Stanley Cup playoffs. Hockey season runs from October–April.

A less expensive option is to go to a college game. Just about every sport conceivable is played at the following colleges in our area:

•San Francisco State University, (415) 338-1111

•San Jose State University, (408) 924-1000

•Santa Clara University, (408) 554-4660

•Stanford University, (415) 723-2300

•University of California at Santa Cruz, (408) 459-0111

•University of San Francisco, (415) 666-6886

ROMANCING MONTEREY

 !!! $$$

The Monterey area is one of the most romantic places in the country. Ocean view restaurants, cute bed and breakfast inns, a variety of outdoor activities, scenic drives, and a friendly community will add up to one wonderful memory. If you need a quick getaway to spend some time together away from the worries of home, Monterey is the place to go.

We have put together a menu of activities for you to choose from. Piece together your own "perfect day" in Monterey with some of these ideas or add in a few of your own. An early start via scenic Hwy. 1 should get you off to a good beginning.

Attractions

• ***Cannery Row***, on historic Cannery Row, Monterey. Formerly a place where sardines were canned by the thousands in the 1940s, Cannery Row now houses a variety of unique shops, ocean view restaurants, and the Monterey Bay Aquarium.

• ***Fisherman's Wharf***, Del Monte Ave., Monterey. Enjoy walking along this weathered pier while browsing at the various gift shops and candy stores. Besides the many wonderful ocean view restaurants at the wharf, you can enjoy watching a variety of boats from whaling vessels to submarines coming into dock. For history buffs, Monterey's Path of History and Maritime Museum are located by the front entrance to the wharf.

• ***Monterey Bay Aquarium***, 866 Cannery Row, Monterey, (408) 648-4888. Located on historic Cannery Row, the Monterey Bay Aquarium features more than 100 galleries and exhibits, including a three story kelp forest and an up close look at sea otters. Open 10 a.m.–6 p.m. daily except Christmas. Admission: $11.25.

Activities

• ***Beaches***. Monterey area beaches are great because they are seldom crowded. We recommend Monterey State Beach (near Fisherman's Wharf) and Carmel Beach on Ocean Ave.

• ***Bicycling***. Rent a bicycle and ride along the Monterey Recreation trail from Fisherman's Wharf to Lover's Point or continue along Ocean View Blvd. Seventeen-mile drive is great in a car, but we do not advise riding bikes along it for safety reasons.

• ***Hiking***. Take a trip down the Big Sur Coast and stop at Point Lobos and Pfeiffer State Park for some of the most beautiful and scenic hikes in the area.

• ***Horseback Riding***. There are few things more romantic than riding a horse across the beach at sunset. If you are interested in taking a scenic drive, travel down the Big Sur Coast to Molera Trail Rides.

• ***Hot Air Ballooning***. Located in nearby Salinas, Balloons by the Sea offers a dramatic view of the valley and Monterey Bay from 3,000 feet up.

• ***Kayaking***. Launching from a small beach off Cannery Row, Adventures by the Sea is the best bet for the novice kayaker. You will be paddling to Lover's Point in minutes and enjoying a closeup view of sea otters and sea lions. Monterey Bay Kayaks launches from Fisherman's Wharf and offers a wide variety of services for the novice and expert kayaker.

• ***Picnicking***. The best two spots for a picnic are Lover's Point Park and Lake El Estero.

• ***Shopping***. If you are in the mood to buy something nice for the one you love, take a look around at one of the following locations:

- ✍ American Tin Cannery Outlet Center (Ocean View Blvd. in Pacific Grove)
- ✍ The Crossroads (Rio Rd. off Hwy. 1 in Carmel)
- ✍ Del Monte Shopping Center (Munras Ave. and Hwy. 1 in Monterey)
- ✍ Downtown Carmel (Ocean Ave. in Carmel)

For the most unique gifts walk through downtown Carmel, and for the best bargains check out the American Tin Cannery.

•***Wine Tasting***. Because Monterey County devotes more acreage to producing wine grapes than any other county in the United States, there are plenty of wineries to choose from. Enjoy a glass a wine at the following locations:

- ✍ Bargetto Winery (700 Cannery Row Ste. L)
- ✍ Chateau Julien (8940 Carmel Valley Rd.)
- ✍ Monterey Peninsula Winery (786 Wave St.)
- ✍ Monterey Wine Company (251 Alvarado Mall)
- ✍ A Taste of Monterey (700 Cannery Row)
- ✍ Ventana Vineyards (2999 Mtry-Salinas Hwy.)

For more detailed information, see our section "Wine Tasting."

Night Life*

• ***Bars.*** There are plenty of small watering holes and classy joints in this town at which to enjoy a drink and the sounds of a live band. Try Franklin St. Bar & Grill (150 W. Franklin), O'Kane's Irish Pub (97 Prescott), and Cibo Restaurant (301 Alvarado).

• ***Dancing.*** There are not a whole lot of choices, but the following clubs offer good music and a comfortable atmosphere: Doc Rickett's (95 Prescott), Brasstree Lounge (Two Portola Plaza), and Nick's Place (180 E. Franklin).

• ***Movies.*** Major theaters are located at the Del Monte Shopping Center (Galaxy 6) in downtown Monterey on Alvarado St. (State Theater),and on Lighthouse Ave. in Pacific Grove (Lighthouse Cinema).

• ***Performing Arts.*** This is not the cultural center of the universe, but you can find some fine plays at California's First Theater located at 200 Pacific St. in Monterey. The Monterey County Symphony puts on six wonderful concerts a year in Carmel and Salinas.

• ***Sports Bars.*** There are two great sports bars in Monterey where you can shoot a game of pool, play darts, or just hang out together in a lively atmosphere: Knuckles Historical Sports Bar (One Old Golf Course Rd.) and Characters Sports Bar (350 Calle Principal).

*For further information on weekly events, pick up a copy of the *Coast Weekly* when you get into town.

Scenic Drives

• ***Hwy. 1 South of Carmel Through Big Sur.*** This is probably the most beautiful scenic drive in all of California. For over an hour, you will enjoy a constant view of the Pacific on your right and rugged mountains and farmlands on your left.

• ***Ocean View Blvd.*** Curve along the Peninsula and enjoy unobstructed views of the ocean, beautiful homes, and deer relaxing on the greens of Pacific Grove Municipal Golf Course.

• ***Scenic Drive.*** This short coastal drive starts near the end of Ocean Avenue and runs parallel to Carmel Beach.

• ***Seventeen-Mile Drive.*** Pass by world class golf courses, landmark spots like the Lone Cypress, and multimillion-dollar homes as you meander from Pacific Grove to Carmel along the coast.

Accommodations

Where you stay depends on what style of hotel you are looking for. There are quaint bed & breakfast hotels and fabulous four star, full service hotels to choose from. Take a look at the section "Romantic Getaways" for information on places to stay in and around Monterey.

Restaurants

Besides San Francisco, there is nowhere else in our region where you can find so many fine places to eat than in the Monterey area. From five-star dining along the ocean to a romantic hideaway tucked in quaint Carmel, finding a nice place to eat is an easy task. Our "Dining Out" section will fill you in on the details.

MOST ROMANTIC DATES

- ✓A sunset bonfire on the beach
- ✓A moonlit carriage ride
- ✓A dinner dance cruise
- ✓Dining in
- ✓Dining out
- ✓Horseback riding on the beach at sunset
- ✓Hot air ballooning
- ✓Romantic getaway
- ✓Weekend getaway

ROMANTIC GETAWAYS

!! $$$$

Going to spend the night at an enchanting, romantic hotel can be like jumping into a giant spa. From the moment you check in, you feel a sense of relaxation. Nice people seem to be everywhere ready to take care of your every need. No matter how perfect life is back home, we all need to go on a little vacation every now and then.

The hotels we have chosen are romantic places to stay in a variety of ways. A good location, attentive and friendly staff, comfortable furnishings, and generous room amenities helped us narrow down the search. But it was the overall feel of the property that counted most. If they could take superb care of a couple out on a romantic holiday, they were selected.

Be sure to make your reservations early, as these are popular hotels. Try a cute bed and breakfast in Monterey one weekend, and perhaps a nice downtown hotel in San Jose or San Francisco next month. Rejuvenate your relationship on a regular basis.

While in town, explore all the community has to offer. Rent some bicycles, picnic in a nearby park, enjoy a fabulous restaurant and take in a show. Check the index to find more suggestions for the city where you are staying.

Twenty Top Romantic Places to Stay

• ***The Archbishops Mansion***, 1000 Fulton St., San Francisco, (415) 563-7872. 15 rooms. Located across from lovely Alamo Square Park, this former home of the Archbishop of San Francisco has been transformed into a 19th-century French chateau. Every room, named after an opera, is uniquely designed with your comfort in mind, including comfortable sitting areas, fireplaces, and serene views. The Carmen Suite ($205) features a beautiful view of the park, a French antique canopied bed, and a clawfoot bath tub set by one of the two fireplaces. A complimentary continental breakfast is delivered to your room in a French picnic basket, and evening wine in the salon. Published rates range from $115–$385. Located near the Civic Center, where opera, ballet, and symphony performances take place.

• ***Babbling Brook Inn,*** 1025 Laurel St., Santa Cruz, (408) 427-2437. 12 rooms. Decorated in a country French style, this charming inn is surrounded by the natural beauty of waterfalls, a meandering creek, and an acre of gardens. Each of the rooms is named after a French Impressionist artist, including the Degas which features a 10-foot-tall white wrought-iron bed from "Romeo and Juliet," fireplace, and a view of the gardens and brook. Guests enjoy a complimentary continental breakfast, afternoon tea and cookies, and evening wine and cheese. Published rates range from $85–$150. Located near hiking and biking trails, downtown Santa Cruz, and the beach.

• ***Cypress Inn***, 407 Mirada Rd., Half Moon Bay, (415) 726-6002. 8 rooms (soon to be 12). You cannot miss the sounds of the ocean when you stay at the Cypress Inn. The beach is just a few steps away from this Santa Fe–style hotel, which will soon feature four new, luxurious suites with every amenity conceivable. Each guest room, named after elements of nature, has an ocean view, private deck, and fireplace. Guests are served a complimentary full breakfast, afternoon tea, and evening wine tasting and hors d'oeuvres. Published rates range from $150–$275. Located minutes from downtown Half Moon Bay.

• ***The Fairmont***, 170 S. Market St., San Jose, (408) 998-1900. 541 rooms. Regarded as the finest hotel between San Francisco and Monterey, the Fairmont offers the ultimate in luxury accommodations and a great downtown location. Step out of the city and into a paradise complete with marble walkways, five fine restaurants, and a private swimming pool among tall palm trees. Guest rooms are well maintained and include generous extras like his and her robes. During the spring and summer, make a reservation for one of their poolside rooms with private verandah. Published rates range from $89–$1,800. Located in the heart of downtown San Jose near several romantic restaurants, the theater, and the light rail.

• ***Garden Court Hotel***, 520 Cowper St., Palo Alto, (415) 322-9000. 61 rooms. With the look of a Mediterranean villa, the Garden Court Hotel has all of the charm of a bed and breakfast hotel and the services of a full-service hotel. Many of the comfortable rooms, with four-poster beds and down comforters, have a terrace that looks out over a garden courtyard or quaint downtown Palo Alto. Their penthouse suite features a fireplace, jacuzzi spa tub, and private sun deck. Guests enjoy complimentary coffee and newspaper each morning. The Garden Courting romance package includes a view room, breakfast in bed, champagne, and extended check out. Published rates range from $175–$425. Located above the fabulous Il Fornaio restaurant in Palo Alto and near Stanford University.

• ***Highlands Inn***, 4 miles south of Carmel on Hwy. 1, Carmel, (408) 624-3801. 142 rooms. Sitting high atop the cliffs, the Highlands Inns best features are the views of Point Lobos and the secluded setting among towering pines. From the spacious lobby and renowned restaurant (Pacific's Edge) to your comfortable guest room, you can enjoy unparalleled views of the ocean. Each room, decorated with warm colors, has a wood-burning fireplace, and all of the suites feature spa baths and kitchens. Published rates range from \$225–\$600. Located near Carmel shopping, beaches, hiking, and horseback riding.

• ***Hyatt Sainte Claire***, 302 S. Market St., San Jose, (408) 295-2000. 170 rooms. Built in 1926 and recently restored to its original European elegance, the St. Claire features comfortable guest rooms with soft colors, feather beds, and generous amenities. Their Plaza Suite includes a king-size sleigh bed, jacuzzi, and dual shower with steam room. Published rates range from \$150–\$945. Located in downtown San Jose and above the wonderful Il Fornaio restaurant.

• ***Inn at Depot Hill***, 250 Monterey Ave., Capitola, (408) 462-3376. 8 rooms. Formerly an old railroad depot, the Inn at Depot Hill was lovingly transformed in 1990 into a luxurious bed and breakfast hotel. Rooms are named after different parts of the world such as Paris, Portofino (Italy), and Delft (Holland). Five of the eight rooms have private patios and outdoor spas, and all of the rooms have wood-burning fireplaces, feather beds, and luxurious modern-day amenities. A complimentary full breakfast, evening wine and hors d'oeuvres, and dessert are served in the dining room or out in their garden amongst roses, azaleas, ferns, and a reflecting pond. Published rates range from \$165–\$250. Located near downtown Capitola and the beach.

• ***Inn at Saratoga***, 20645 Fourth St., Saratoga, (408) 867-5020. 46 rooms. Located just off the main street of quaint Saratoga, the Inn at Saratoga is a peaceful romantic hideaway with all of the amenities. Attractively decorated modern rooms each have their own private balcony overlooking Saratoga Creek and Wildwood Park. A complimentary continental breakfast is served in their luxurious lobby. Published rates range from \$145–\$495. Located near wineries and the Hakone Japanese Gardens.

• ***The Majestic***, 1500 Sutter St., San Francisco, (415) 441-1100. 57 rooms. Originally built in 1902, the recently furbished Majestic hotel displays a rich Victorian/Edwardian style including four-poster canopy beds and French and English antiques. Their romance package includes a grand deluxe suite with large bay window, fireplace, champagne and chocolates, and dinner for two in the romantic Cafe Majestic. All guests enjoy a complimentary continental breakfast (weekdays) and sherry and biscotti from 4–5 p.m. Published rates range from $125–$250. Located in a quiet residential area just two blocks from the cable car line.

• ***Mill Rose Inn***, 615 Mill St., Half Moon Bay, (415) 726-9794. 6 rooms. You may be convinced you have found the Garden of Eden as you look past their white picket fence into a beautiful, multicolored rose garden. Eve Baldwin, one of the owners, has a smile that will brighten up your day as much as the plentiful arrangements of flowers scattered about the inn. Besides the standard amenities at most hotels, your room will include complimentary sherry, a stocked minibar, Japanese robes, romantic board games, and even "flip-flops" for a walk to their enclosed, outdoor spa for two. Five of the rooms have a fireplace and every room has a private door to the relaxing garden patio. The Bordeaux Rose Suite ($265), with canopy bed and whirlpool tub, is very romantic. A complimentary breakfast and afternoon tea and cookies are served in the dining room. Published rates range from $165–$265. Located near the restaurants and shops of Half Moon Bay and the beaches.

• ***Monterey Plaza Hotel***, 400 Cannery Row, Monterey, (408) 646-1700. 285 rooms. Located on Steinbeck's historic Cannery Row and overlooking the ocean, the Monterey Plaza offers luxurious headquarters in romantic Monterey. Their guest rooms are large and spacious and many have balconies with a view of the Monterey Bay. Having just completed a five- million-dollar renovation, the property has never looked better. Published rates range from $150–$275. Located near Lover's Point Park and Fisherman's Wharf.

• ***Old Monterey Inn***, 500 Martin St., Monterey, (408) 375-8284. 10 rooms. This grand English Tudor inn sits on over an acre of beautifully landscaped gardens including a variety of shade trees, traditional English hedges, and a magnificent rose garden. All rooms have sitting areas, feather beds, and goose down comforters and pillows. A complimentary full breakfast, evening wine and hors d'oeuvres, and soft drinks and coffee are served daily. The large Ashford Suite has a fireplace and a lovely view of the garden. Published rates from $170–$240. Located in a quiet residential neighborhood near downtown Monterey.

• ***The Prescott Hotel***, 545 Post St., San Francisco, (415) 563-0303. 166 rooms. Built in the early 1900s and recently renovated, the Prescott features lovely Edwardian-style guest rooms with all of the modern-day amenities. Across from the hotel's inviting living room with its country hearth–style fireplace is Wolfgang Puck's Postrio restaurant, where hotel guests receive preferential seating. All guests receive complimentary morning coffee and tea, evening wine and cheese in the living room, and a newspaper. The Mendocino Penthouse Suite ($700) features a formal dining room, rooftop jacuzzi, and two wood-burning fireplaces. Published rates range from $195–$215 for a deluxe guest room and $245–$265 for a deluxe suite. Located near theaters, Union Square, and cable car line.

• ***Seven Gables Inn***, 555 Ocean View Blvd., Pacific Grove, (408) 372-4341. 14 rooms. The attention to detail in this 109-year-old Victorian is phenomenal. From the collection of fine European, Oriental, and American antiques to the Persian carpets, crystal chandeliers, and stained-glass windows, the right setting has been created. Every room has an ocean view, and each has been decorated with elegance, comfort, and romance in mind. The Cypress Room ($185) has a 180 degree, unobstructed view of the ocean and unique features including a sculpted medallioned ceiling and stained-glass windows. A complimentary full breakfast and afternoon tea are served in the lobby. Published rates range from

$105–$205. Located near Cannery Row, downtown Pacific Grove, and Lover's Point.

• ***The Sherman House***, 2160 Green St., San Francisco, (415) 563-3600. Well known as one of the most romantic places to stay in the area, the Sherman House will sweep you off your feet into the luxury and comfort of a Victorian mansion. Decorated in a French-Italianate style, rooms feature canopied feather beds, wood-burning fireplaces, and splendid views. The Sherman Suite has its own large private terrace that provides a sweeping view of the Bay from the Golden Gate Bridge to Alcatraz Island. Published rates range from $190–$825. Located just one block from the many shops on Union Street.

• ***Stonepine***, Carmel Valley Rd. 13.3 miles east of Hwy. 1, Carmel Valley, (408) 659-2245. 14 suites. Stonepine is in a class by itself. This secluded, 330-acre Estate Ranch sits in the heart of sun-kissed Carmel Valley surrounded by rolling green hills and magnificent oaks. Eight large, comfortable suites are located in the main house (Chateau Noel) including the Taittinger which has a fireplace, marble bath and jacuzzi, and a hidden staircase that leads to a huge living room overlooking the grounds. On property you will find an equestrian center, hiking trails, archery range, croquet, tennis courts, swimming pool, health club, and formal dining room. A complimentary breakfast and evening champagne and hors d'oeuvres are served in the living room. Published rates range from $225–$750.

• ***Ventana***, 28 miles south of Carmel on Hwy. 1, Big Sur, (408) 667-2331. 60 rooms. Ventana can be best described as the best romantic escape in California. If you are looking to get away from civilization and spend some quality time together, you will find nothing but peace and tranquility at this four-star country inn resort. From your private deck and hammocks scattered about, you can enjoy views of the ocean, grassy meadows, and a canyon dotted with majestic redwoods. Most rooms, decorated with cedar and wicker, have fireplaces and a few have fireplaces, and a hot tub. The large Canyon Townhouse Suites have a wood-burning fireplace and views of both the ocean and the canyon. A complimentary breakfast and afternoon tea are served in their lobby. Published rates range from $195–$880. Located near Pfeiffer Beach, Pfeiffer State Park for hiking, and Molera Trail Rides for horseback riding.

• ***The Warwick Regis Hotel***, 490 Geary St., San Francisco, (415) 928-7900. 80 rooms. Walking into the Warwick Regis will transport you from modern-day San Francisco to the days of Louis XVI. Each room has a four-poster or crown canopy bed, antique English or French armoire, and Italian marble baths. For serious lovers only, this hotel has a romance package that includes a deluxe room, champagne, a regis memento, and breakfast in La Scene Cafe. Every guest enjoys a complimentary continental breakfast and newspaper. Published rates range from $105–$205. Located near theaters, Union Square, and the cable car line.

• ***White Swan Inn***, 845 Bush St., San Francisco, (415) 775-1755. 26 rooms. This traditional English inn, built just after the great quake of 1906, is very charming and comfortable. The central living room area, with comfortable couches and chairs, features two fireplaces, a library, and a garden patio. All of the spacious guest rooms have fireplaces, and all guests are treated to a complimentary full breakfast, cookies and tea in the afternoon, and a champagne reception every Thursday. They have two "Romance Suites" and a celebration package that includes champagne and a cuddly teddy bear to take home. Published rates range from $145–$250. Located above Union Square and below Nob Hill near the cable car line. *Note: The **Petite Auberge**, run by the same management group, is also very nice and is located just a few doors down.*

SAN FRANCISCO ADVENTURE

 !!! $$$

Appropriately referred to as "The City," San Francisco is consistently voted as one of the top destinations in the world. There are few places where you can find so much to do and see in such a small area. Stretching from the foot of the Golden Gate to the edge of the county line, San Francisco is less than 50 square miles in size.

San Francisco is probably most recognized for its landmarks such as the Golden Gate Bridge, Coit Tower, and the Forty-Niner football team. What brings the people inside the city borders, though, ranges from the beauty of Golden Gate Park, restored Victorian mansions, and enchanting North Beach to the excitement of Broadway shows and electric night clubs. Most importantly, San Francisco is also a city of romance with cute boutique inns, intimate restaurants, and breathtaking vistas.

We have listed below a sampling of things to do and places to see in San Francisco. You will find that one weekend is not long enough, so make sure to return to the city by the Bay again and again.

Attractions

• ***Alcatraz Island***. Access from the ferries departing from Pier 41. Originally a Civil War fort and later a federal penitentiary, Alcatraz is now a national park. You can visit some of the old jail cells, and "the yard" and get a feel for what it was like on "the rock."

• ***Angel Island***. Access from the ferries departing from Pier 41. A beautiful island with plenty of places to picnic, hike, and bike.

• ***Cable cars***. Lines run along California, Powell, Washington, Jackson, Hyde, and Mason Sts. A distinctive symbol of San Francisco, this unique method of transportation will take you to Fisherman's Wharf, Nob Hill, and Union Square in style.

• ***Chinatown***. Grant and Stockton Sts. from Bush St. to Broadway. One of the largest Chinese-American communities in the country, Chinatown encompasses buildings with Chinese architecture, fresh seafood markets, wonderful restaurants, and shops featuring everything from souvenir and herb shops to silk blouses and ivory carvings.

• ***Civic Center***. Van Ness Ave. from Turk St. to Hayes St. The Civic Center area has a handsome collection of French renaissance buildings including City Hall, War Memorial Opera House, Veterans Building and Davies Hall. City Hall, with its grand staircase and rotunda, is modeled after our nation's capitol and is quite spectacular.

• ***Coit Tower***. On top of Telegraph Hill Blvd. off Lombard St. Erected in 1933 as a memorial to the firefighters who battled the fires after the 1906 quake, Coit Tower offers spectacular views of the city and the bay from 210 feet up.

• ***Fisherman's Wharf and Pier 39***. Jefferson St. One of the area's biggest tourist attractions, there are plenty of souvenir and specialty shops and seafood restaurants. A streetside gallery of attractions including the Wax Museum, Q-Zar laser tag, and Ripley's Believe It! or Not is located across the street from the wharf.

• ***Ghirardelli Square***. North Pt. and Polk St. This small shopping complex, located near the waterfront, offers attractive boutiques, fine restaurants, and specialty shops including the Ghirardelli Chocolate Factory and The Sharper Image.

• ***Golden Gate Bridge***. From Hwy. 101 and Hwy. 1 north leading over the Bay to Marin County. Opened in 1937, this 4,200-foot-long suspension bridge is one of the largest in the world. Take a 50 minute walk over the Pacific on the Golden Gate Bridge and enjoy some unforgettable views of the city, bay and Alcatraz Island.

• ***Golden Gate Park***. Bordered by Fulton St., Lincoln Way, Stanyan St., and the Great Hwy., (415) 666-7200. The park comprises over 1,000 acres including grassy picnic areas, wooded walking trails, several lakes, and scenic bike routes. Attractions inside the park include the California Academy of Sciences, deYoung Museum, Asian Art Museum, Japanese Tea Garden, Conservatory of Flowers, Strybing Arboretum, and Shakespeare Garden.

• ***Japantown***. Bordered by Geary Blvd., Sutter St., Laguna St., and Fillmore St. Within this three block area you will find a combination of restaurants, art galleries, and shops offering all sorts of wonderful items from the Orient.

• ***Lake Merced***. Harding Rd. and Skyline Blvd., (415) 753-1101. Nature trails, golf courses, and bicycle trails surround Lake Merced, which offers windsurfing, rowboating, and paddleboating.

• ***Lombard Street***. Between Hyde and Leavenworth Sts. Known as "the crookedest street in the world," this one block section of

Lombard spirals downward on a brick paved pathway at a 40-degree slope.

• ***North Beach***. East of Columbus St. from Washington St. to the Wharf. Home of San Francisco's Italian community, North Beach features Italian restaurants, coffeehouses, delicatessens, jazz clubs, and lovely inns. Near the center of North Beach are Washington Park and the majestic Church of Saints Peter and Paul.

• ***Union Square***. Bordered by Post, Stockton, Geary, and Powell Sts. Located in the heart of downtown San Francisco, this is one of the best places to shop, with every major department store and specialty store imaginable nearby.

Activities

• ***Bay Cruise***. From large ferry boats to luxury yachts, you can sail to just about anywhere. See the section "Cruising the Pacific" for more information.

• ***Beach***. Ocean Beach, located along the Great Hwy., is a great place to walk along but too windy to enjoy a picnic or suntan. Try hiking down to China Beach or Baker Beach.

• ***Bicycling***. Ride along the northern coast at the Land's End Trail, through Golden Gate Park, or take your bike across the Golden Gate Bridge and enjoy unparalleled views of the bay.

• ***Hiking***. Take a walk along the many trails of Golden Gate Park or along the coast to inviting views of the Golden Gate Bridge.

• ***Picnic***. Two of the best spots are Golden Gate Park and the Marina Green, which is located on Marina Blvd. near the ocean, Fisherman's Wharf, and the Presidio. See page 97 for more details.

• ***San Francisco Zoo***. Sloat Blvd. and the Great Hwy. Ranked as one of the top city zoos in the country, the San Francisco Zoo features over 1,000 animals, including a rare white tiger, polar bears, and penguins. Gorilla World, the Lion House, the Insect Zoo, and the Primate Discovery Center are some of the favorite exhibits.

• ***Shopping***. The best shopping can be found at Union Square, the Union Street Shops (Union between Steiner and Gough), San Francisco Shopping Centre (865 Market St. at 5th), Stonestown Galleria (19th Ave. at Winston), and Embarcadero Center (Clay and Sacramento Sts. between Battery and Drumm).

• ***Sporting Events.*** Catch a Giants game or a Forty Niner game out at Candlestick Park or a college game at the University of San Francisco and San Francisco State University.

Nightlife

• ***Bars***. From the crowded pubs of North Beach to the lofty bars in downtown, there are plenty of places to go for good music and drinks. Try Gordon Biersch Brewery (2 Harrison St. at Steuart), Hard Rock Cafe (1699 Van Ness at Sacramento), Top of the Mark (19th floor of Mark Hopkins Hotel), Harry's (2020 Fillmore St. at California), and Johnny Love's (1500 Broadway at Polk).

• ***Comedy Clubs.*** San Francisco features some of the nation's finest comedy entertainers at Cobb's and The Punch Line.

• ***Dancing***. A great variety of dance clubs in San Francisco are located south of Market Street and include Harry Denton's, Club Oasis (11th at Folsom), DNA Lounge (11th at Harrison), and Slim's (11th at Folsom).

• ***Performing Arts***. The best in theater, opera, symphony, and ballet can be found in San Francisco. See our section "Performing Arts" for more details.

Scenic Drives

The 49-mile scenic drive takes you through the city to some of the best vistas in San Francisco including Telegraph Hill, Twin Peaks, and Golden Gate Park. Just follow the white signs along the road marked with a seagull and the number 49.

Accommodations

San Francisco has hundreds of hotels ranging in rates from $29 to $2,000 a night. There are many romantic boutique hotels located all over the city as well as four- and five-star full service hotels in the heart of downtown. Decide what you might want to do in San Francisco and then find a hotel that is near those activities. Take a look at the section "Romantic Getaways" for some suggestions.

Restaurants

With so many diverse communities, San Francisco offers some of the best international dining to be found. Our "Dining Out" section will steer you to a few of the most romantic places to eat.

SCENIC DRIVES

!! $

One way to top off a perfectly romantic day or evening is to take a scenic drive around the area. As you wind through the mountains, beside the ocean, or along the outskirts of the city, you will be rewarded with some breathtaking views. If you can, stop along the route, share your thoughts and a kiss, and enjoy the view.

If you are driving during the day, you can surprise your date by packing a picnic lunch or snack and serving it at one of several vista points along the way. In the evening, stop to watch the sunset or gaze out over the city lights. When you finally head home, pop in a tape of your date's favorite songs and enjoy the drive back.

Ten Scenic Drives

• ***Forty Nine Mile Drive***, San Francisco County. Access from Van Ness St. at Fulton and head north following the signs marked with a seagull and the number 49. This long drive through the city passes by the Civic Center, Union Square, Coit Tower, Fisherman's Wharf, Ghirardelli Square, the Presidio, Golden Gate Park, Ocean Beach, and Lake Merced, to name just a few spots. The best scenery is offered by taking ***Twin Peaks Blvd***. up to the top, where you will enjoy a panoramic view of all of San Francisco.

• ***Hecker Pass Hwy.*** (Hwy. 152 West), Santa Clara and Santa Cruz Counties. Access from Hwy. 1 via Hwy. 129 in Watsonville or from Hwy. 101 near Gilroy. A beautiful mountain road that winds through fields, majestic redwoods, wineries, oak-studded hills and past Mount Madonna Park.

• ***Hwy. 1 from Monterey through Big Sur***, Monterey County. Access from Hwy. 1 starting near the Del Monte Exit. Pass by the Monterey Bay and Carmel on your way to the most beautiful stretch of coastline in California. The drive along the Big Sur Coast features magnificent views of the Pacific, Santa Lucia Mountains, beaches, and a variety of cow and horse-studded pastures.

• ***Hwy. 1 from Pacifica to Santa Cruz***, San Mateo and Santa Cruz Counties. Access from Hwy. 1 heading south of San Francisco or north from Santa Cruz. Hugging the ocean and going past several beaches, this spectacular drive offers the best views of the coast during the day. On your journey, you will pass by the city of Half Moon Bay, Pigeon Point Lighthouse, and Big Basin Redwoods State Park. *Note: Road is subject to closure.*

• ***Hwy. 9 from Downtown Saratoga to Skyline.*** Access from Hwy. 17 to Hwy, 9 or Hwy. 280 to Saratoga/Sunnyvale Rd. to Hwy. 9. Start with a drive through lovely downtown Saratoga and leave civilization behind as you wind up to Skyline Ridge. Pass by the Hakone Japanese Gardens, several wineries, and Sanborn-Skyline Park on your way to a vista point with a commanding view of the Santa Clara Valley.

• ***Hwy. 92*** west toward Half Moon Bay, San Mateo County. Access from Hwy 280. and Hwy 1. at Half Moon Bay. A short highway route that winds up and down the mountains with scenic views of the valley, several Christmas tree farms, and colorful nursery flowers before reaching the town of Half Moon Bay and the ocean.

• ***Seventeen Mile Drive and Ocean View Blvd,*** Monterey County. Access from Hwy. 1 south to Hwy. 68 (Pebble Beach Gate). Wind along the ocean on this historic drive and pass by world-class golf courses, several scenic landmark locations, Asilomar Beach, and multimillion-dollar homes. Continue out the Pacific Grove exit and follow Ocean View Blvd. around the bay to Lover's Point Park.

• ***Skyline Blvd.*** (Hwy. 35), San Mateo and Santa Cruz Counties. Access from Hwy. 280 to Hwy. 92 toward Half Moon Bay and from Hwy. 17 to Summit Road (west). For over 60 miles you will enjoy a variety of views, including the Santa Cruz Mountains, Christmas tree farms, county parks, Silicon Valley, the ocean, giant redwoods, and San Francisco. It is like escaping from civilization for a couple of hours.

• ***Stevens Canyon Rd.***, Santa Clara County. Head west on Stevens Creek Blvd. and turn left on Foothill Blvd. (which becomes Stevens Canyon Rd.). Wind through the hills on heavily wooded backroads and enjoy views of Stevens Creek Park and Reservoir. Continue left onto Mt. Eden Rd. and right onto Pierce Rd. to view some multimillion-dollar homes before arriving in Saratoga.

• ***West Cliff Dr./Beach St. from Natural Bridges State Beach to Santa Cruz Beach Boardwalk***, Santa Cruz County. Access from Hwy. 17 south to Hwy. 1 north. Turn left onto Swift St., right onto Delaware Ave., and left on Swanton Blvd. to W. Cliff. Follow this short trek along the ocean through Lighthouse Field State Beach and stop at the Boardwalk.

LEAST EXPENSIVE DATES

✓Beach
✓Bicycle Adventures
✓Coffeehouses
✓Fairs & Festivals
✓Hiking
✓Ice & Roller skating
✓Kids for a day
✓Miniature golf
✓Physical Activities
✓Picnics
✓Romantic movie rental
✓Wine tasting

SPORTS BARS

♡ !! $

If you and your significant other love sports, you will definitely enjoy yourselves at a sports bar. From the moment you walk through the front door, you will be struck with images of Joe Montana and "The Catch," Mark McGwire and Barry Bonds blasting home runs, and Tim Hardaway taking it to the hoop.

Sitting at the bar or at a table, you are surrounded by televisions carrying many games from several different sports. Even if you are not rooting for one of the hometown teams, you can watch and cheer for your team thanks to the wonders of satellite television.

Besides watching the games on television, enjoying good old-fashioned American cuisine and a beer, most sports bars have a pool table, a dart board, and a variety of other games like foosball, air hockey and arcade games. Watch a few games, play a few games, and enjoy the lively atmosphere found in a sports bar.

Sports Bars

• ***America's Original Sports Bar*** at San Jose Live!, 150 S. First St., San Jose, (408) 294-5483.

• ***Bank Shot Sports Bar***, 350 Altair Way, Sunnyvale, (408) 733-3855.

• ***Duffy's Sports Cafe***, 219 B&C Mt. Hermon Rd., Scotts Valley, (408) 438-6627.

• ***Halftime***, 675 El Camino Real, Palo Alto, (415) 473-0945.

• ***Knuckles Historical Sports Bar***, Hyatt Regency Monterey, One Old Golf Course Rd., Monterey, (408) 372-1234.

• ***Knuckles Historical Sports Bar***, Hyatt Regency San Francisco Airport, Burlingame, (415) 347-1234.

• ***Lefty O'Douls***, 333 Geary at Powell, San Francisco, (415) 982-8900.

• ***Pat O'Shea's***, 3848 Geary at 3rd St., San Francisco, (415) 752-3148.

• ***Sneakers***, 1163 San Carlos Ave., San Carlos, (415) 802-0177.

• ***Sports City Cafe***, Saratoga-Sunnyvale Rd. and Hwy. 280, Cupertino, (408) 253-2233.

THRILLING ACTIVITIES

♡ !!!! $$$

If you are in the mood to go a little over the edge and do something out of the ordinary, then keep reading. The businesses listed below are ready to make you jump, bounce, and fly through the air.

Hang gliding, parasailing, bungee jumping and skydiving all share one thing in common—they let you experience flying. Whether it be for just seconds or many minutes, you will either float on a cushion of air or experience free fall for hundreds of feet.

With all of these daredevil "sports," there is an emphasis on instruction. Your safety must come first. If you are not ready, then do not go until you feel adequately prepared. There is a little danger involved, but life itself is dangerous. You will experience something not soon forgotten.

Bungee Jumping, Hang Gliding, Skydiving, & Parasailing

• ***Bridge Bungee Jump***, (408) 855-9143. They offer bungee jumps off bridges into a river or anything else you can dream up that is safe. Cost is $90 per person for two jumps each. Bungee outings approximately one time every three weeks.

• ***Pacific Parasailing***, on Santa Cruz Wharf, Santa Cruz, (408) 423-3545. Flights over the northern edge of the Monterey Bay take place during the spring and summer. Please call ahead for information.

• ***Skydive Hollister***, 55 Mercury Dr., Hollister, (408) 636-3483. After four to five hours of ground training, most people are ready for a free fall jump accompanied by two instructors. Accelerated free fall jumps are $270. After about 15 minutes of training, you can do a tandem jump with an instructor pulling the chute for $160. Call at least a day or two ahead of time for reservations. Jumping takes place from 8:30 a.m.–sunset every day except Tuesday and Thursday.

• ***Western Hang Gliders***, Hwy. 1 at Reservation Rd., Marina, (408) 384-2622. They offer a beginning course for only $89 that includes a three hour course, including classroom time, ground school, and at least five low-level flights. Complete lesson packages range from the $89 package to the Eagle Package at $1,295. Call for availability.

WEEKEND GETAWAYS

!!! $$$$

We are so fortunate to be located near several fantastic vacation getaways. We have chosen some of the most romantic and exciting places to spend a weekend together. Whether you are interested in just relaxing or being extremely active, these destinations will not disappoint you.

The driving times range from only one to five hours. To start your vacation a little earlier, consider taking a train, bus, or plane. This way you will not have to worry about driving and can enjoy the scenery along the way.

Pack lightly and take a spontaneous approach to your vacation. Whatever you do, do not become a slave to a schedule that has you doing just about everything possible in one short weekend. Read through our suggestions, figure out what you might want to do, and if you find the time, then do it.

Santa Barbara

Tucked away between the Santa Ynez Mountains and the Pacific Ocean, Santa Barbara is a California paradise commonly referred to as "The American Riviera." Although the geography of the area is similar to that of the French Riviera, there is a strong Spanish and Mexican influence from days gone by in the city's long history.

There is always something to do in Santa Barbara, and with sun and comfortable temperatures all year round, everything is possible just about any time. Perhaps that is why so many celebrities make this their vacation home.

Directions

Located five hours south of San Francisco on Hwy. 101. If you would prefer not to drive, take the Amtrak Train, (800) 872-7245, or a commuter flight into Santa Barbara Airport.

Attractions

• ***Arts and Crafts Show***, Cabrillo Blvd. near Chase Palm Park. Every Sunday the local artists and craftspeople display their works along Cabrillo Blvd. from Stearns Wharf along the East Beach. The show begins at 10 a.m. and ends around sunset.

• ***Botanic Garden***, 1212 Mission Canyon Rd., (805) 563-2521. Take a walk through 65 acres of lush gardens and enjoy a wide variety of California's native flora from the deserts, the Sierra Nevada, and the southern mountains. Open daily from 9 a.m. to sunset. Admission: $3.

• ***Santa Barbara Museum of Art***, 1130 State Street, (805) 963-4364. One of the finest small museums in California, the Santa Barbara Museum of Art includes works by Monet, Matisse, and Degas as well as Asian art, photographs, contemporary art, and modern European art. Open Tuesday–Sunday from 11 a.m.-5 p.m. Admission: $3.

• ***Stearns Wharf***, on State St., (805) 564-5518. The oldest operating wharf on the West Coast, Stearns Wharf is a great place to buy a few souvenirs, browse the seafood markets, and enjoy lunch or dinner at one of the fabulous ocean view restaurants. A main attraction on the wharf is the Sea Center which offers a look at local marine life.

• ***Zoological Gardens***, 500 Ninõs Dr. off Cabrillo Blvd., (805) 962-5339. Between the 700 animals and beautiful botanic gardens, there is plenty to see and experience at this zoo. Enjoy a picnic, ride their miniature train, or relax in their restaurant.

Open daily from 10 a.m.-5 p.m. (summers from 9 a.m.-6 p.m.) Admission: $5.

Activities

• ***Beaches.*** With the town skirting the edge of the Pacific, you do not need to look far for the beach. The most popular beaches are the East Beach and West Beach, both located near the Stearns Wharf.

• ***Biking***. Rent a bicycle and take an easy three mile ride along the waterfront path or a longer ride along the Cabrillo Bikeway. For bike rentals, contact Beach Rentals (805-963-2524 near the Wharf) or Open Air Bicycles (805-963-3717 on Chapala St. downtown).

• ***Boating***. A variety of boating opportunities are available including dinner cruises, coastal sailing excursions, island trips, kayak rentals, and whale watching trips. Contact one of the following businesses: AKA Sunset Kidd's Charters (208-962-8222 for sailing, harbor cruises and island trips), Captain Don's Harbor Tours (805-969-5217 for sunset cruises and whale watching), Sailing Center of Santa Barbara (805-962-2826 for boat rentals, coastal cruises, dinner cruises, whale watching and island excursions), Santa Barbara Aqua Sports (805-564-8815 for kayak rentals and island tours) and Sea Landing Aquatic Center (805-963-3564 for dinner cruises and whale watching).

• ***Hiking***. With the Santa Ynez Mountains shadowing Santa Barbara, there are several hiking trails that will give you tremendous views of the valley and ocean below. The Cold Spring Trail is one of the best. Also check out the Channel Islands for several spectacular all day hiking opportunities.

• ***Horseback Riding***. Stables at a variety of locations offer rides along the beach and through the mountains from early morning to the sunset hours. For information contact Circle Bar B Riding Stables (805) 968-1113, San Ysidro Stables (805) 969-5046, or Goleta Valley Community Stables (805) 968-2024.

• ***Picnicking***. There are several beautiful parks in the city that are perfect for picnicking. They include the Alice Keck Park Memorial Garden (Micheltorena and Santa Barbara Sts.), Shoreline Park (La Marina and Shoreline Dr.) and Alameda Park (1400 Santa Barbara St.).

• ***Shopping***. The downtown area features several shopping areas selling anything from antiques and paintings to designer clothes and gourmet foods. Take a walk up and down State St. and you will find six different complexes.

• ***Wine Tasting***. Within Santa Barbara County are 30 wineries, most of which are gracious enough to offer a complimentary tasting. Within downtown Santa Barbara are two tasting rooms: Santa Barbara Winery (202 Anacapa St.) and Stearns Wharf Vinters (217 Stearns Wharf). For a detailed touring map of the wineries, contact the Vintners' Association at (805) 688-0881 or check with the hotel concierge.

Scenic Drives

• ***Scenic Drive*** through Santa Barbara. This self guided driving tour of the area weaves through the foothills of the Santa Ynez Mountains, past the opulent residential communities, and past 16 points of interest in the downtown area and along the waterfront.

Accommodations

The following are guides to accommodation rates:
$$: under $100; $$$: $100-$150; $$$$: Over $150.

• ***Chesire Cat Inn***, 36 W. Valerio St., Santa Barbara, (805) 569-1610. $$$

• ***Fess Parker's Red Lion Resort***, 630 E. Cabrillo Blvd., Santa Barbara, (805) 564-4333. $$$$

• ***Montecito Inn***, 1295 Coast Village Rd., Montecito, (805) 969-7854. $$$

• ***San Ysidro Ranch***, 900 San Ysidro Ln., Montecito, (805) 969-5046. $$$$

• ***Simpson House Inn***, 121 E. Arrellaga St., Santa Barbara, (805) 963-7067. $$

• ***Villa Rosa Inn***, 15 Chapala St., Santa Barbara, (805) 966-0851. $$

Restaurants

• ***Citronelle***, E. Cabrillo Blvd. and Milpas St. at the Santa Barbara Inn, Santa Barbara, (805) 966-2285.

• ***The Harbor Restaurant***, 210 Stearns Wharf, Santa Barbara (805) 963-3311.

• ***Stonehouse Restaurant***, 900 San Ysidro Ln. at the San Ysidro Ranch, Montecito, (805) 969-5046.

• ***The Wine Cask***, 813 Anacapa St., Santa Barbara, (805) 966-9463.

Sonoma Valley

Take a trip to the quiet side of the wine country by visiting nearby Sonoma Valley. Unlike the Napa Valley, where you may find crowds of people wine tasting up and down Hwy. 29, in the Sonoma Valley you can explore a more rural area that is quite peaceful.

The town of Sonoma, located in the heart of Sonoma Valley, has a rich history dating back to the early 1800s. In the town's Sonoma Plaza you can explore ancient adobes, historic wineries and visit the site of the famous Bear Flag Revolt of 1846. Besides the historical flavor of the town, there are several good restaurants, interesting shops, and romantic inns.

Directions

From Hwy. 101 north past San Francisco, take Hwy. 37 to Hwy. 121 to Hwy. 12 into the downtown area of Sonoma. The drive is approximately one hour from San Francisco, two hours from San Jose, and three hours from Monterey.

Attractions

• ***Sears Point International Raceway***, Hwy. 37 at Hwy. 121, (707) 938-8448. One of the state's primary racing facilities, they offer exciting motorcycle and auto racing most weekends.

• ***Sonoma Cheese Factory***, 2 Spain St., (707) 938-5225. A delectable variety of cheeses including the famous Sonoma Jack Cheese can be purchased here. You can also just watch them make the cheese from scratch. Open daily from 9 a.m.–6 p.m.

• ***Sonoma Mission***, Spain and First Sts., (707) 938-1578. Built in 1823 as the last of California's 21 missions, the Sonoma Mission defines the area's rich history with displays and paintings. Cost: $1. Open daily from 10 a.m.–5 p.m.

• ***Sonoma Plaza***, located at the center of town. From this central location, you can walk to the old adobes and tour around this busy little town. Afterwards, pick up a few deli items at the Sonoma Cheese Factory and the Sonoma French Bakery. Find a picnic spot in the beautiful park located in the center of the plaza and relax by the duck pond or rose garden.

• ***Train Town***, 20264 Broadway south of the Plaza, (707) 938-3912. Feel like a kid again as you take a 20 minute train ride through this theme park, passing through tunnels and under bridges Cost: $2.20. Call for availability.

Activities

• ***Hiking***. Several trails can be found at Jack London Historic State Park (open daily from 8 a.m.–sunset) and at Sugarloaf Ridge (open daily from sunrise–sunset).

• ***Horseback Riding***. The Sonoma Cattle Company (707-996-8566) offers guided tours through Jack London Historic State Park and Sugarloaf Ridge State Park for only $22 for two hours.

• ***Hot Air Ballooning***. Take a flight over the Sonoma Valley in a hot air balloon with Sonoma Thunder (707-996-3665) or Air

Flamboyant (707-575-1989). Each company offers a package for $145 per person including a champagne brunch.

• ***Picnics***. Besides Sonoma Plaza, you can picnic in the beauty of the wilderness of Jack London State Historic Park (London Ranch Rd., [707] 938-5216) or Sugarloaf Ridge State Park (2605 Adobe Canyon Rd., [707] 833-5712). Most of the wineries above also have lovely picnic areas where you can enjoy your meal with a nice bottle of wine.

• ***Spas***. The most heard about spa retreat has to be the Spa at Sonoma Mission Inn off Hwy. 12 (707-938-9000). They offer every sort of spa treatment from massage and facial to a soak in their natural hot mineral water pools. For a less expensive option, try the Sonoma Spa on the Plaza (707-939-8770) for massage, mud treatments, and herbal facials.

• ***Wagon Tours/Carriage Rides***. Tour the wine country in a horse-drawn wagon (Wine Country Wagons, [707] 833-2724) or enjoy a carriage ride through Jack London State Historic Park (Sonoma Cattle Company, [707] 996-8566).

• ***Wine Tasting***. There are a wide variety of wineries located all over the Sonoma Valley. Near the edge of town, check out two of the oldest California wineries at Sebastiani (Fourth and E. First Sts., est. 1904) and Buena Vista Winery (18000 Old Winery Rd., est. 1857). Other fantastic wineries to sample wine at are as follows:

- ✍ Chateau St. Jean, 8555 Sonoma Hwy, (707) 833-4134. Open daily from 10 a.m.–4:30 p.m.*
- ✍ Glen Ellen Winery, 1883 London Ranch Rd., (707) 935-3000. Open daily from 10 a.m.–4:30 p.m.*
- ✍ Gloria Ferrer Champagne Caves, 23555 Hwy. 121, (707) 996-7256. Open daily from 10:30 a.m.–5 p.m.

✍ Gundlach-Bundschu Winery, 2000 Denmark St., (707) 938-5277. Open daily from 11 a.m.–4:30 p.m.

✍ Hacienda Wine Cellars, 1000 Vineyard Ln., (707) 938-3220. Open daily from 10 a.m.–5 p.m.

✍ Kenwood Vineyards, 9592 Sonoma Hwy., (707) 833-5891. Open daily from 10 a.m.–4:30 p.m.*

✍ Ravenswood Winery, 18701 Gehricke Rd., (707) 938-1960. Open daily from 10 a.m.–4:30 p.m.

✍ St. Francis Winery, 8450 Sonoma Hwy., (707) 833-4666. Open daily from 10 a.m.–4:30 p.m.*

✍ Valley of the Moon Winery, 777 Madrone Rd., (707) 996-6941. Open daily from 10 a.m.–5 p.m.*

✍ Viansa, 25200 Arnold Dr. (Hwy 121), (707) 996-7256. Open daily from 10a.m.-5p.m.

(Note:* denotes wineries found on or just off of Hwy. 12).

Accommodations

The following are guides to accommodation rates:
$$: under $100; $$$: $100-$150; $$$$: Over $150.

• ***El Dorado Hotel***, 405 First St., Sonoma, (707) 996-3030. $$

• ***Gaige House Inn***, 13540 Arnold Dr., Glen Ellen, (707) 935-0237. $$$

• ***The Hidden Oak***, 214 E. Napa, Sonoma, (707) 996-9863. $$

• ***Kenwood Inn***, 10400 Sonoma Hwy., Kenwood, (707) 833-1293. $$$$

• ***Sonoma Mission Inn and Spa***, 18140 Hwy 12, Sonoma, (707) 938-9000. $$$$

• ***The Thistle Dew Inn***, 171 W. Spain St., Sonoma, (800) 382-7895. $$$

• ***Trojan Horse Inn***, 19455 Sonoma Hwy., Sonoma, (707) 996-2430. $$$

Restaurants

• ***Babette's***, 464 First St. E., Sonoma, (707) 939-8921.

• ***Eastside Oyster Bar and Grill***, 133 E. Napa St., Sonoma, (707) 939-1266.

• ***Ristorante Piatti***, 405 First St. W. at the El Dorado Hotel, Sonoma, (707) 996-2351.

• ***Sonoma Mission Inn Grille***, 18140 Sonoma Hwy. at Boyes Blvd., Sonoma, (707) 938-9000.

South Lake Tahoe

You usually hear a lot about the Lake Tahoe area during the ski season. As winter approaches, we are given daily updates on snowfall and ski conditions and some friendly advice about carrying chains. With the ski resorts just a few hours from San Francisco, it is impossible to stay away.

Although many people come to this mountain paradise for snow skiing, there is something for everyone in South Lake Tahoe at any time of the year. From summer hiking and biking along the lake to gambling along the glitzy casino strip, people of all ages come to this area for a nice little getaway.

Directions

From Hwy. 280 north in San Francisco, take Interstate 80 east until you reach the junction at Hwy. 50. Follow Hwy. 50 east into South Lake Tahoe. You can also fly into the South Lake Tahoe Airport via American Airlines (800-433-7300) or TWA (800-221-2000) or you can take Amtrak.

Attractions

• ***Casino District***. On Hwy. 50 just past the state line into Nevada. Even if you do not gamble, this is where you will find a lot of activity. Harvey's, Harrah's, Caesar's, and the Horizon Casino

Resort offer gambling and a wide variety of entertainment including Las Vegas–style shows, comedy, and major music performances.

• ***Emerald Bay State Park***. Off Hwy. 89 about 10 minutes north of South Lake Tahoe. Located at the head of Emerald Bay is the Viking castle named Vikingsholm. Tour this twentieth century 38-room castle and believe that you have traveled through time to centuries long ago. Emerald Bay, one of the most photographed areas in the world, also offers a variety of scenic hikes and picnic areas.

• ***Heavenly Valley Aerial Tram***. Heavenly Valley Ski Resort, 1261 Ski Run Blvd., (916-541-1330 and 916-541-7544). Take a thrilling one-mile ride from 2,000 feet up over the Gunbarrel ski run. The views of the lake and the mountains cannot be matched.

Activities

• ***Beaches***. Relax by the lake at one of South Shore's great beaches including Baldwin Beach (off Hwy. 89), Regan and El Dorado Beaches (Hwy. 50 to Lakeview), and Kiva Beach (off Hwy. 89).

• ***Biking***. Two of the most popular bike paths are the Pope-Baldwin Bike Path along Hwy. 89 toward Emerald Bay and the South Lake Tahoe Bike Path starting at Hwy. 50 near the South Lake Tahoe Recreation Area Beach.

• ***Carriage/Sleigh Rides***. Borges Carriage & Sleigh Rides (916-541-2953) will bring you through the snow in one and two horse open sleighs. It is a very romantic experience.

• ***Gambling***. Amidst the beauty of South Lake Tahoe is a half-mile-long gambling district featuring Harrah's, Harvey's, Caesar's, and the Horizon Casino Resort. From the bell ringing slots to the soft roll of the dice, gamblers can be delighted 24 hours a day.

• ***Hiking***. Lake Tahoe is surrounded by thousands of square miles of forest and a host of scenic hiking trails. Venture out to the U.S. Forest Service Lake Tahoe Visitors Center (916-541-5255), Emerald Bay State Park, Sugar Pine Point State Park (916-525-7982), and the Desolation Wilderness Area (916-573-2600) for a variety of trails for all skill levels.

• ***Horseback Riding***. Their are several stables located near the lake that offer hourly rentals, sunset rides, and pack trips. Contact Camp Richardson's Corral (916-541-3113), Cascade Stables (916-541-2055) or Zephyr Cove Stables (702-588-5664).

• ***Lake Cruises***. Forget about jet skis and speedboats and step aboard one of South Lake Tahoe's two Mississippi-style paddlewheelers. The Tahoe Queen (916-541-3364) and M.S. Dixie II (702-588-3508) offer daily cruises in picturesque Emerald Bay as well as sunset dinner dance cruises.

• ***Picnicking***. Try the beaches we mentioned above or for a more rustic feel travel to D.L. Bliss State Park (off Hwy. 89 north of town) and picnic under the pines.

• ***Skiing.*** The two major downhill ski areas in the South Lake Tahoe area are Heavenly Valley (916- 541-1330) and Kirkwood Ski Resort (209-258-3000). Heavenly Valley is the largest alpine ski area in the country, and Kirkwood receives some of the heaviest snowfall in the area.

• ***Snowmobiling***. If there is snow on the ground and you do not feel like skiing, try an exciting ride on a snowmobile. Contact Snowmobiling Unlimited (916-583-5858).

• ***Water Sports***. Check out the marinas at Lakeside (916-541-6626), Ski Run (916-544-0200), Timber Cove (916-544-2942), Tahoe Keys (916-541-2155) and Zephyr Cove (702-588-3833) for rental and launch information for motorboats, sailboats, jet skis, kayaks, and fishing boats. The lake is even more beautiful when you are on it!

Scenic Drives

• ***Around Lake Tahoe***. Take the spectacular 72-mile drive around Lake Tahoe on Hwys. 89, 28, and 50 and see Emerald Bay, Cascade Lake, Tahoe City, Crystal Bay, and many wonderful and unique views of the lake.

• ***Kingsbury Grade***. From Nevada Rte. 207 off of Hwy. 50, drive up the Kingsbury Grade (7,375 feet at the summit) and then quickly descend into the Carson Valley. The views of Lake Tahoe and Carson Valley are quite spectacular.

Accommodations

The following are guides to accommodation rates:
$$: under $100; $$$: $100-$150; $$$$: Over $150.

• ***Caesar's Tahoe***, Lake Tahoe Blvd., South Lake Tahoe, (702) 588-3515. $$$

• ***Christiani Inn***, 3819 Saddle Rd., South Lake Tahoe, (916) 544-7337. $$

• ***Embassy Suites***, 4130 Lake Tahoe Blvd., South Lake Tahoe, (916) 544-5400. $$$

• ***Inn by the Lake***, 3300 Lake Tahoe Blvd., South Lake Tahoe, (916) 542-0330. $$$

• ***Tahoe Seasons Resort***, Keller and Saddle Rds., South Lake Tahoe, (916) 541-6010. $$$

Restaurants

• ***Christiania Inn Restaurant***, 3819 Saddle Rd., (916) 544-7337.

• ***Evan's***, 536 Emerald Bay Rd., (916) 542-1990.

• ***Fresh Ketch***, 2435 Venice Dr. E., (916) 541-5683.

• ***Llewellyn's***, At Harvey's Resort, (702) 588-2411.

WHALE WATCHING

♡ !! $

Imagine cruising on the Pacific in search of a nature experience unlike any other. Standing outside on the deck of a large touring boat, you can feel the cold winds coming off the ocean. Suddenly, the boat cuts its powerful engines and quietly comes to a stop. The captain, binoculars in hand, shouts, "Thar she blows!"

You are never quite sure what you are going to run into on a whale watching tour. Sometimes it will be the sight of a large gray whale migrating to or from Baja. Perhaps you will be fortunate enough to experience firsthand the mating ritual of the blue whale. Sometimes, dolphins will pass by in sync with the boat so close you can nearly touch them.

Whale watching cruises take place mostly in the winter and during a few of the summer months. Because of the limited amount of trips, please make your reservations early. The best times to go in our area are January and February. After your expedition, stop off at a local cafe and warm up with a nice cup of coffee.

Whale Watching Tours

• ***Tom's Sportfishing***, Sandholdt Rd., Moss Landing, (408) 633-2564. Departing only once a day, you will enjoy a multiple-hour cruise that continues for as long as there are whales in sight. Cost: $15.

• ***Randy's Fishing Trips***, 66 Fisherman's Wharf #1, Monterey, (408) 372-7440. They offer a two-hour narrated cruise to see the whales as they migrate from Alaska to Baja. Cost: $14.

• ***Santa Cruz Sportfishing***, H-Dock, Upper Harbor, Santa Cruz, (408) 426-4690. Observe the majestic gray whales migrating to and from Baja on this three hour cruise. Cost: $16.

• ***Monterey Sportfishing and Cruises***, 96 Fisherman's Wharf #1, Monterey, (408) 372-2203. Cruise on the largest boats on the bay and enjoy watching the California grays in the winter and humpbacks, orcas, blues and dolphins in the summer. Cost: $12–$15 (winter), $25 (summer).

• ***Oceanic Society Expeditions***, San Francisco and Half Moon Bay, (415) 474-3385. Led by expert naturalists, the Oceanic Society offers whale watching tours nearly all year round. December–April is the gray whale migration and in June–November are Farallon Islands natural history excursions for humpback and blue whales. Trips depart from San Francisco December–November and from Half Moon Bay from December–April. Cost: $32-$58.

WINE TASTING

♡♡ !! $

Half the fun of wine tasting is your trip to the wineries and tasting rooms. In this part of the state, there really is not one stretch of road where you will find more than a few good wineries near each other. You will need to travel to different areas ranging from the mountains of Santa Cruz to the valleys of Gilroy. Each place offers a beautiful, unique setting in which to enjoy a glass of wine.

What if you do not know a lot about wine? Who cares! Go out and enjoy the beautiful countryside, talk with interesting people, and learn a little about what distinguishes a cabernet from a merlot. When you have finished tasting a variety of wines, spend some time picnicking, perhaps on a grassy knoll overlooking acres of sun-kissed vines. Most wineries also offer tours of the property as long as you make prior arrangements.

Please be careful not to taste too much wine and then drive. We suggest visiting only a few wineries at a time in one central area.

Key:

[C] = complimentary wine tasting

[P] = picnic areas

[T] = winery tours available

Twenty Great Places to Go Wine Tasting

Santa Cruz Area

• ***Bargetto Winery***, 3535 N. Main St., Soquel, (408) 475-2258. At this oldest of the Santa Cruz Mountain wineries, tranquillity can be found in their charming courtyard overlooking Soquel Creek. Tasting offered Monday–Saturday from 9:30 a.m.–5 p.m. and Sunday from Noon-5 p.m. [C] [T]

• ***Bonny Doon Vineyard***, 10 Pine Flat Rd., Santa Cruz, (408) 425-3625. Located in the Santa Cruz Mountains, their tasting room is located in a building known by locals as "The Lost Weekend Saloon." Lovely picnic facilities are located within a redwood grove alongside Mill Creek. Call ahead for tasting times. [C] [P] [T]

• ***Devlin Wine Cellars***, 3801 Park Ave., Soquel, (408) 476-7288. This small winery, set by an expansive lawn surrounded by redwood trees and a flowered knoll overlooking Capitola and the Monterey Bay, offers the best picnicking opportunities Wine tasting offered weekends from Noon–5 p.m. [C] [P]

• ***Hallcrest Vineyards***, 379 Felton Empire, Felton, (408) 335-4441. Hallcrest features organically grown, organically processed wines at their historic winery located in the heart of the Santa Cruz Mountains. Enjoy a picnic out on the deck overlooking the vines and Henry Cowell Redwoods State Park. Wine tasting offered daily from 11 a.m.–5:30 p.m. [C] [P] [T]

Monterey Area

• ***Chateau Julien,*** 8940 Carmel Valley Rd., Carmel, (408) 624-2600. Housed in a French country-style chateau, this winery sits east of Hwy. 1 in the majestic Carmel Valley. Wine tasting offered Monday–Friday from 8:30 a.m.–5 p.m., Saturday and Sunday from 11 a.m.–5 p.m. [C] [T]

• ***Monterey Peninsula Winery,*** 786 Wave St., Monterey, (408) 372-4949. This small tasting room, offering a variety of table wines, is conveniently located one block up from the Monterey Bay Aquarium and Cannery Row. Tasting offered daily from 11 a.m.–5 p.m. [C]

• ***A Taste of Monterey,*** 700 Cannery Row, Monterey, (408) 646-5446. This 7000-square-foot wine tasting room offers a sampling from 23 Monterey County wineries. You can enjoy Monterey wines, local produce plates or appetizers, and a spectacular panoramic view of the ocean. Wine tasting offered daily from noon–6 p.m. Cost: $2 charge for 3 tastes.

• ***Ventana Vineyards,*** 2999 Monterey-Salinas Hwy. (68), Monterey, (800) BEST-VIN. This award winning winery is not the most scenic place to go wine tasting, but trying their variety of experimental wines is well worth the trip. Wine tasting offered daily from 11 a.m.–5 p.m. [C] [P]

Gilroy Area

• ***Fortino Winery***, 4525 Hecker Pass Hwy., Gilroy, (408) 842-3305. Located in a beautiful valley near Mount Madonna Park, the Fortino complex includes a gift shop, a garlic gourmet shop, and a full-service Italian deli. Wine tasting offered daily from 10 a.m.–5:30 p.m. [C] [P] [T]

• ***Kirigin Cellars,*** 11550 Watsonville Rd., Gilroy, (408) 847-8827. Located in the Uvas Valley just miles from the wineries on Hecker Pass, the winery sits on the historic Solis Rancho Homestead in buildings dating back to 1827. Ask to try their "kissing wine." Wine tasting offered daily from 10 a.m.–5 p.m. [C] [T]

• ***Solis Winery,*** 3920 Hecker Pass Hwy., Gilroy, (408) 847-6306. This quaint winery, surrounded by a beautiful lawn and garden area, has a tasting room that overlooks acres of vines. Wine tasting offered Wednesday–Sunday from 11 a.m.–5 p.m. [C] [P]

• ***Thomas Kruse Winery***, 4390 Hecker Pass Rd., Gilroy, (408) 842-7016. A small, rustic winery where you are sure to run into friendly Thomas Kruse hard at work. Besides their great, inexpensive wines you will enjoy looking at his eclectic collection of antique winemaking equipment. Open daily from noon–5 p.m. Cost: $1 wine tasting fee refundable with purchase. [P] [T]

Los Gatos/Saratoga Area

• ***Byington Winery,*** 21850 Bear Creek Rd., Los Gatos, (408) 354-1111. Located high atop the Santa Cruz Mountains, Byington Winery offers views across the redwood forests down to the Monterey Bay from their picnic area. Wine tasting offered daily from 11 a.m.–5 p.m. [C] [P] [T]

• ***David Bruce Winery,*** 21439 Bear Creek Rd., Los Gatos, (408) 354-4214. Overlooking the San Lorenzo Valley and Monterey Bay, this winery has quietly become one of our area's most respected wine makers. Wine tasting offered Wednesday–Sunday from noon–5 p.m. [C] [P]

• ***Mariani Vineyards,*** 23600 Congress Springs Rd., Saratoga, (408) 741-2930. This historic winery, built in 1912, is tucked away in the Santa Cruz Mountains among towering redwoods. Wine tasting offered daily from 11 a.m.–5 p.m. [C] [P] [T]

• ***Mirassou Champagne Cellars***, 300 College Ave., Los Gatos, (408) 395-3790. Located at the site of the historic Novitiate Winery in the Los Gatos hills, Mirassou features award-winning sparkling wines. Tasting offered Wednesday–Sunday from noon–5 p.m. [C] [T]

Salinas Valley

• ***Jekel Vineyard***, 40155 Walnut Ave., Greenfield, (408) 674-5522. The most southern of the Salinas Valley wineries, Jekel sits on the valley floor with pretty views of the hills that surround the vineyard. Open daily from 9:30 a.m.–4 p.m. [C] [P] [T]

• ***The Monterey Vineyard***, 800 S. Alta St., Gonzales, (408) 675-2316. This modern winery is located in a beautiful complex surrounded by acres of grass, a small pond, and picnic areas. Their tasting room is large and offers an opportunity to purchase deli items and wine souvenirs. Wine tasting daily from 10 a.m.–5 p.m. [C] [P] [T]

• ***Paraiso Springs Vineyard,*** 38060 Paraiso Springs Rd., Soledad, (408) 678-0300. Come sample a variety of wines from their scenic tasting room overlooking the Salinas Valley. Tasting offered Monday–Friday from noon–4 p.m., Saturday and Sunday from 11 a.m.–5 p.m. [C] [P]

• ***Smith and Hook Winery*** and ***Hahn Estates***, 37700 Foothill Rd., Soledad, (408) 678-2132. Their tasting room, high atop the mountains overlooking acres of vines and the Salinas Valley, is located inside an enormous wine barrel. Wine tasting offered daily from 11 a.m.–4 p.m. [C] [P] [T]

MOST UNUSUAL DATES

✓Day at the races
✓Dining in
✓Hot air ballooning
✓Kids for a day
✓Limousine tours
✓Murder mystery dinner theater
✓Thrilling activities

"THANKS FOR A GREAT TIME"

The sweetest words you can hear after a date are "Thanks for a great time." It doesn't matter if these words come from a "blind date," a second date, or your spouse: they still sound great. How good a time people have when they are out with you can greatly depend on where you go.

Throughout this book we have listed dates that are good for a variety of situations. For instance, going out for coffee on a first date is not a bad idea. It gives you a chance to talk and get to know each other. A comedy club would also be a great idea because of the relaxing environment that will help "break the ice" between you.

Now, if you were to prepare a romantic dinner back at your place for a first date, you could scare off the other person who might wonder: What are your intentions? Why are you getting so serious so quickly? Maybe this wasn't such a good idea.

If you are celebrating a special occasion, your date probably will not appreciate just a cup of coffee. Maybe you will need to spend a little money to go on an unforgettable romantic adventure like a chartered sunset cruise, hot air ballooning, or away for the weekend. Special occasions are special because they do not happen very often. Treat them with loving care.

What if you are a little short on cash? No problem. There are a lot of things to do for under $10 per couple. With a little creativity and thought, a trip to the beach can be one of the most romantic times you ever have. For a more casual date, check out some of the biking and hiking trails around the area— the cost is almost nothing.

Different people like different things. If you know the person you are dating loves the outdoors, do something outdoors. Your date will have more fun and appreciate your consideration of what they enjoy.

Whatever you are looking for, this book can be of great use to you if you keep it from collecting dust on the bookshelf. Carry it in the car when you go out. Keep it in front of you as a reminder that there are plenty of fun, exciting, and romantic places to go and things to do in this area.

Personal Choices

In the spaces provided below, fill in your own personal favorites for some of the activities detailed in this book. Keep a good record so that you can visit these places time and time again.

When you have had the chance to really use this book, send us a copy of your personal choices. If we use one of your new ideas, your name will appear on the acknowledgment's page of our next edition (a chance to become famous!).

Beaches

____

____

____

Bicycle Adventures

____

____

____

Carriage Rides

____

____

____

Coffee Houses

____

____

____

Comedy Clubs

Concerts

Cruising the Pacific

Dancing

Dining In

Dining Out

Fairs & Festivals

Hiking

Horseback Riding

Hot Air Ballooning

Ice & Roller Skating (incl. outdoor paths)

Kayaking

Kids for a Day

Limousine Tours

Miniature Golf

Movies

Performing Arts

Picnics

Romancing Monterey

Romantic Getaways

San Francisco Adventure

Scenic Drives

Sports Bars

Thrilling Activities

Weekend Getaways

____
____
____

Whale Watching

____
____
____

Wine Tasting

____
____
____

New *Fun, Exciting & Romantic Places*

____
____
____
____

****

Name:______________________________________
Address:____________________________________
______________________Phone: ( ) ____________
How did you hear about this book? ______________
___________________________Age (optional): _____

*To request another Personal Choices form, please contact us in writing at 540 N. Santa Cruz Ave., Ste. 152, Los Gatos, CA. 95030.

INDEX

ABOUT THE AUTHOR

The publisher and author, Brian Borgia, graduated from Santa Clara University with a degree in marketing and a dream of writing this book. For the past seven years, he has worked in the travel and hospitality industry in cities stretching from Palo Alto to Monterey. During this time, he has had the opportunity to sell our wonderful destination to people all over the world. He has lived (and dated) in this region for over 26 years and currently resides in Monterey.